THE VI[...]

Gideon Haigh is a Melbourne journalist and author of the award-winning cricket biography *Mystery Spinner: The Story of Jack Iverson*.

BY THE SAME AUTHOR

The Battle for BHP

The Cricket War: The Inside Story of Kerry Packer's World Series Cricket

The Border Years

One Summer, Every Summer: An Ashes Journal

Australian Cricket Anecdotes

The Summer Game: Australian Test Cricket 1949–71

One of a Kind: The Story of Bankers Trust Australia 1969–99

Mystery Spinner: The Story of Jack Iverson

The Big Ship: Warwick Armstrong and the Making of Modern Cricket

The Vincibles
A Suburban Cricket Season

GIDEON HAIGH

TEXT PUBLISHING
MELBOURNE AUSTRALIA

The Text Publishing Company
171 La Trobe Street
Melbourne Victoria 3000
Australia

Copyright © Gideon Haigh 2002

All rights reserved. Without limiting the rights under copyright above, no part of this publication shall be reproduced, stored in or introduced into a retrieval system, or transmitted in any form or by any means (electronic, mechanical, photocopying, recording or otherwise), without the prior permission of both the copyright owner and the publisher of this book.

Published in the UK in 2002 by Aurum Press as *Many a Slip: A Diary of a Club Cricket Season*

Printed and bound by Griffin Press

Typeset in 12.5/16 Garamond 3 by J & M Typesetting

National Library of Australia
Cataloguing-in-Publication data:

Haigh, Gideon.

The vincibles : a suburban cricket season.

ISBN 1 877008 35 4.

1. South Yarra Cricket Club - Humor. 2. Cricket - Victoria - South Yarra - Humor. I. Title.

796.35862099451

FOR THE BOYS

A Yarras Preamble

This is a short book about a small cricket club with an unremarkable history and an uncertain future. It behoves me to make this clear at the outset. Low expectations minimise disappointment—or so I have found as a player.

The club, the Yarras, is the one to which I belong. And the club to which you belong is always different, special, unique. Outsiders simply don't understand. Which may be for the perfectly sound reason that they lead complete and fulfilling personal and professional lives, have close-knit families and wide circles of long-standing friends, and thus no reason to be interested in anything so base and plebeian as the rituals of male companionship—but, well, what do they know anyway, eh?

My involvement with South Yarra Cricket Club spans nine years. When I arrived, it was as a fill-in for what was billed as the Third XI. I say 'billed' because, while Third was nominally accurate, XI was pure hype—there were seldom more than eight of us. The team tended to be a bit of an afterthought. The chief skill of its players was that of rationalising failure, like the proverbial Collingwood supporter dismissing a defeat by 'twenty lucky goals'. Times, fortunately, have changed a bit since then. We now field four XIs—although the Fourths can sometimes be a bit XI-ish. We have a pretty ground, excellent club rooms and a working fridge—even if they're not actually ours. It's not rags-to-riches, but it is rags-to-better-quality-rags.

Over the last four years, I've become involved in duties off-field. The management of the Yarras is like that of most clubs. It is run—for want of a better word—by its committee. The committee is elected—again for want of a better word—by the players. And the committee—for want of any word that really describes it accurately—does stuff. Or at least, stuff gets done. We pay a curator to tend our pitches, but all other duties are delegated either to the first volunteer or the last person to rule themselves out. Being somewhat slow in the latter respect, I now occupy the roles of vice-president, chairman of selectors, newsletter editor, karaoke impresario, trivia quizmaster and club greyhound shareholder. This may seem quite a lot, but the responsibilities are surprisingly manageable, providing you don't expect to work for a living between the months of September and March. And freelance journalists are accustomed to that.

What follows, then, traces the Yarras' fortunes during the season of 2001–2. It is in the form of a diary (à la Steve Waugh), though it occurs to me that a journal kept during any other season would read very similarly (also à la Steve Waugh). We won some, lost some, played in scorching sun and driving rain—this being Melbourne, sometimes on the same day. We had exciting partnerships (occasional), middle-order collapses (traditional), tail-end disintegrations (habitual). We struck mountainous sixes then ran each other out, took miraculous catches then dropped complete gobbers, beat the edge with inch-perfect outswingers then claimed wickets with outrageous dibbly-dobblies (good job, that). And we were broke. As traditions go this is probably the most enduring.

This is also a book about the sort of cricket where it doesn't really matter if you're any good, providing you're good enough. When people find out I'm still a participating cricketer, one of their first questions is: 'What's the standard like?' This I find hard to answer. It's fair to say that nobody at the Yarras is on John Buchanan's speed dial. Some of our bats are bare of stickers, but that's because they're old, not because we're awaiting Microsoft's offer. Bourkey has a haircut like Warnie's, though he drives a ute not a Ferrari, and if he chatted up a nurse in a nightclub it would make the *South Yarra Sentinel* rather than a London tabloid. And Wogger is a regular in the VIP area at Melbourne's casino, but only because he throws drunks out of it, not because he's in cahoots with John the Bookie.

Standards, however, are relative. And at the level of cricket we play, I suspect they're ultimately meaningless. I mean, it's not like any of us are going anywhere in a hurry. You sometimes hear boosterists describe Australian cricket as a 'pyramid', at whose apex repose those irresistible Men-o-Waugh, and at whose base are the swarming undifferentiated millions for whom a weekly game might be the first step on a brilliant career. This is useful for propaganda purposes, but would scarcely withstand close inspection.

Cricket in Australia is better imagined as a ziggurat, and a rough-hewn, misshapen one at that: full of cricketers who've stopped off part-way through their ascent to enjoy the view, full of guys serious about the game but less so about their games. If the ambition for achievement was ever there, it's long been phased out in favour of the objective of disgrace-avoidance. Keats coined the expression 'negative capability' to describe the state in which 'a man is capable of being in uncertainties, mysteries, doubts, without any irritable reaching after fact and reason'. The weekend cricketer understands this: he's got a weakness outside off stump, has always had it, is quite used to it, and even kinda likes it.

Not that we're landlocked in mediocrity, and don't hanker to do well; of course we do. I feel I get more value from cricket than, say, Mark Waugh does. He'll never derive as much satisfaction as I do from stroking a ball through extra cover, because he does it well, and I don't. He expects to hit the ball where he intends. For me, there remains the enchantment of surprise. It's simply that the pleasure of park cricket is broader than runs, wickets and catches. It has to be.

One aspect of the Yarras appeals to me most of all. South Yarra is a pretty chi-chi suburb, at least by reputation and rateable property values. But a quirk of the cricket club members playing under its name is that nobody lives anywhere near South Yarra. Players arrive because they've a friend or a friend of a friend who happens to lure them down. Players stay because they want to. It is, in the old-fashioned sense, a club—a voluntary assembly rather than a civic amenity. Our common thread is that we enjoy the cricket and the company. This doesn't mean that the Yarras are particularly special; the world is full of cricket clubs, each unique in history and tradition, quality and character. They're simply special to me.

Week 1

Committee

September is always a good month at the Yarras. Everyone's keen and nobody's played; a few of us haven't even cleaned our whites from last season yet. We wonder aloud whether this might be *our season*. Disillusionment can wait until after Round One at least.

But before a ball can be bowled in anger—or in tranquillity—there must be meetings, further meetings, and meetings about the need for further meetings. This can be tiresome, as the Yarras committee traditionally finds no issue too minor for interminable debate; choosing the cordial flavour for drinks breaks has been like negotiating the Treaty of Ghent. Talk is cheap—making it one of the few activities in which we can freely engage.

A few years ago we had a president I shall call Lombard—Lots Of Money But A Real Dickhead—who insisted that every aspect of club affairs be regularised in a series of charters: committee charter, players' charter, captains' charter, selection charter et al. In a fit of misplaced whimsy, I proposed a barbecue charter and lengthy deliberations ensued about a gas bottle roster and maintenance of the burger tab. It was like joining the People's Front of Judaea.

Our first confab of 2001–2, though, is different. The state-of-the-Yarras address by TB, our president, departs from tradition with the announcement that he's had a vasectomy that morning and remains in some discomfort. For the rest of the evening, time-consuming detours in discussion are arrested by his reminder: 'Pain, guys.' Seven pairs of legs cross and uncross in sympathy.

TB is an able president: wise, benevolent, a *soi-disant* 'schmoozer'. In civilian life, he's a marketing executive at a computer company, which is sometimes detectable in his language. 'Can you action that?' or, 'Can you take ownership of that process?' he'll say. But he also has a strange capacity for talking you into things. For all I know, the vasectomy may be a cunning ploy to expedite the committee process. On second thoughts, no: he really does look like a man trying to hatch an egg.

Under this new dispensation, planning our first social function is a breeze. We're holding a traditional Australian festive occasion—watching the Brownlow Medal telecast. Pub or club rooms? Club rooms. Big TV or little TV? Big. Beer or beer? Yep. 'Let's go up-market,' suggests Panther. 'How about we order pizzas?' No anchovies? Motion carried; one abstention (president in toilet).

Next item: chairman of selectors, i.e. who will be this season's sucker? I squirm a little in my seat, having been last season's sucker, and having announced my unconditional, irrevocable and perpetual non-candidature in a 'You-won't-have-Nixon-to-kick-around-anymore' farewell address at our presentation night in April.

I'll explain. Being Yarras' chairman of selectors is like hosting a talkback radio program where you actually have to do something about the callers' problems rather than just tell them to shut up, get a job or write to their MP before hanging up on them.

Because their problems are yours.

Consider a standard conundrum: Bill can only play every third Sunday or else his workers' compensation insurers might guess that he's not paralysed from the waist down; Bob can't play every third Sunday because he's having an affair with Bill's wife, who's sick of her husband pretending to be paralysed. On second thoughts that's easy: they can take turns playing, with the club, and with Bill's missus. But you get the picture.

Hey, hang on. All eyes have swivelled in my direction. 'The president might have had a vasectomy,' I protested, 'but what makes you think I've had a lobotomy?' Too late, I'm surrounded. 'Yeah,' I grumble. 'All right.' Mulva, unanimously elected as club secretary a few months ago while holidaying in Bali, enters my unanimous election as chairman of selectors in the minutes with a satisfied smirk. Fat Tony the treasurer asks, 'Where did you get that scar on your forehead?'

One of our most distinguished ex-players, Fat Tony then reports on club finances. This is always a bit of a strain. We could fund our club on the loose change in Steve Waugh's pockets. But to do so, we would have to find his dry cleaner, apply for a job, work our way up to a level of responsibility in the organisation so that we were trusted with Steve Waugh's suits, then rifle his pockets in search of the copious coinage he doubtless possesses. And this plan fails on a number of levels—such as that none of us likes ironing.

Fat Tony's report sounds like an inventory of Old Mother Hubbard's cupboard; our financial limits seem perfectly limitless. I study the uncomfortable grimaces round the table, not least TB's—leaning forward out of more than eagerness to grapple with the issue.

'The situation's a bit worrying,' says Fat Tony, which is worrying in itself. Fat Tony usually takes a Micawberesque view of the club accounts: he only intervenes when the bar credit reaches three times consolidated revenue. But as he explains, while having no money is merely a bummer, having association registration fees of $600 due at the same time is a major bummer indeed.

Womble, our delegate, points out an irony. The association is offering $1400 interest-free loans to clubs purchasing new covers. 'Pity we bought our covers last season,' he laments, describing a rare instance of committee foresight.

Expressions change. 'An interest-free loan?'

'Yes, for a year.'

'And all you need is covers?'

'Yes, which we've got.'

'That sounds like a win-win: we'll borrow the money to pay the association from the association.'

Suddenly, we're geniuses again. It's the sort of accounting entrepreneurship that made the Skase and Bond empires great. Better still, we'll have a spare $800. Punting money. A club jacuzzi. A Scandinavian masseuse. And new players. 'We're going to buy a premiership!' announces Panther.

Proceedings close with debate over whether Adam Gilchrist or Glenn McGrath will make the better recruit. Like I said, September is a month of hope. It's gotta be *our season*.

Week 2

Pre-Season

Were it in my power, I'd decree that the cricket season last twelve months of the year—not only because I enjoy the game, but because of the effort involved in starting again after a winter's inactivity. The ball seems absurdly small, and hard. The bat feels like an ill-fitting prosthesis. In the nets pitches telescope to 100 yards when you're bowling, then truncate to ten yards when you're batting. And your hands are so soft it seems like you've been washing dishes for the last six months: in fact, if you've been trying to butter up a wife or girlfriend ahead of your frequent absences over the coming season, this might actually be the case.

Fortunately, at pre-season training everyone's in the same boat; in fact, it's a veritable USS *Enterprise* of incompetence. While football retains dominion over our Como Park home ground, we train weekly—undercover at Hawthorn Indoor Cricket Centre. This isn't ideal as the run-ups are brief and the carpet surfaces benign. But the arrangement does hold one significant advantage: nobody else can see us.

The happiest aspect of pre-season training is, of course, getting back together with everyone. All the old incorrigibles turn up. First to arrive is Womble. He's always first, brimming with enthusiasm, bursting with words. He's a modest cricketer but the only guy I've met who can make an innings of 9 on Saturday last all week as a monologue subject. I'd guess on writing quite a bit about Womble in coming months, mainly because I'll be listening to him quite a bit.

Quieter is Hicksy, at fifty-one our oldest player, with a quarter-century at the Yarras behind him. He arrives in his van, the Bog Roll Express (he is, in civilian life, a toilet paper salesman). We're both offies, and refer to ourselves privately as 'the Spin Sisters'. Our greeting is now time-honoured:

'G'day Sis.'

'G'day Sis.'

'Turning any?'

'Nope.'

'Good. Hate to be the only one.'

My longest-standing crony is Rhino, a roundhead bat and wrong-foot medium-pacer, with whom I played in my very first game. I proudly MC'd his wedding earlier this year, and marriage seems to have agreed with him. He leaves his first hit for the season streaming with sweat. 'That's one pizza down,' he confides. 'Only forty-three to go.'

Everyone lights up when Moof saunters in, with the shoulder-rolling gait of a boisterous toddler. He's our best young all-rounder and most irrepressible piss-taker. I've just written a book about Warwick Armstrong, *The Big Ship*, and he wants me to know that he's seen it on the shelves in Borders.

'I trust you didn't buy it or anything silly like that,' I inquire.

'No,' he says. 'But it was obviously in the wrong place. I put it back in the shipping section.'

As ever, the biggest contingent to arrive are the clannish Maccas: brothers Pete, Dave, Steve and Rod. They're a distinctive Australian feature of the club, continuing a lifelong backyard Test in the environs of the Yarras, hitting hard, bowling bouncers and bagging one another. Pete Macca and Dave Macca are captains of our Firsts and Seconds respectively this season and it will be interesting to see if the politics of the communal bedroom re-emerge at the selection table. They're already arguing about Matthew Lloyd's suspension for head-butting. Promising.

I have a hit on the bowling machine, and strike the ball surprisingly well—mind you, I often do at this stage of the season, ahead of a six-month form lapse. My looking in no discomfort is also a mistake because Womble, who's feeding the contraption, soon gets bored. After serving up a series of welcoming half-volleys, he programs a wicked outswinger, which I miss by about a yard. 'Oh, that was a beautiful delivery!' he chortles delightedly. 'Unplayable! You were lucky not to get a touch on that!' Then helpfully, 'I'll give you a few outswingers now.'

I'm just beginning to adapt to these when a smoking in-ducker slams into my boot. 'Howzat!' Womble exults. 'Gone! Yes, that's plumb. Off you go.' Then: 'I'm going to switch to inswingers now.'

I look down and amazingly my foot still seems attached. I hobble into line for the next few balls until a steepling bouncer zooms past my throat. Womble is laughing so much he can hardly form words. 'What a great ball!' he snorts. 'That almost killed you! Fantastic!' Pause. 'I'll start dropping them a bit shorter now.' And so on.

At the first training, twenty guys turn up, which is pretty good at a time of year in Melbourne when it's Aussie Rules finals. And, despite the general air of lassitude, a few players already look sharp. Among the new faces is Kinger, a strapping young left-arm quick (mental note to avoid his net this summer). Moof then cracks Wogger's box in half with an off-cutter (ditto). CC is also quite a handful. He's been known to go whole seasons without making a delivery bounce on a pitch, but indoors he can be formidable: not only do his parabolae turn off the roof of the net, but you end up with sore eyes from trying to spot the ball out of the fluorescent lighting.

So we're back. And it still feels fun, which is always a concern before any reunion with bat and ball. The skills—or what skills you have—will come back to you in due course. But will your enjoyment have survived the hiatus? For a professional cricketer, the issue of enjoyment can't have the same resonance. What the hell else is he going to do? Translate Homer? Design cathedrals? But for an amateur, enjoyment means everything. We don't have to do what we do.

I've just read Philip Roth's *Great American Novel*, and liked the passage when big, baseball-loving Luke Gofannon was asked by his girlfriend if he loved her as much as he loved triple plays. 'I can't tell a lie, Angela,' he said. 'There just ain't nothin' like a triple.' As long as something similar runs through my head before each season, I'll be content. Sad, sad bastard.

Week 3

Selection

Thursday night at the Yarras is selection night—after a fashion. Teams aren't so much picked as move into alignment like celestial bodies. We work around the usual range of absences, ailments, preferences, excuses. Then there's our own profound disorganisation.

At the start of each season, the player contact list is a freewheeling combination of fact and fiction. You e-mail the wicketkeeper and his wife replies; although it's now his ex-wife, who's busy burning his gear in the backyard. You ring the last number you had for the left-arm spinner, and end up on a pizza parlour's hotline; so you order a Mexicana with extra cheese, which fills a hole, but not that hole in the Third XI.

Typical is the season's first meeting to draft our

four XIs, involving the four captains, Pete Macca (Firsts), Dave Macca (Seconds), Doc (Thirds), Churchyard (Fourths) and myself. Attendance rolls studiously marked at training to keep track of new arrivals cause widespread bemusement. 'Does anyone know who Mark Warren is?' I ask. Shrugs from the skippers. 'Well, he's been to training four times, so he's obviously keen.' Fourths? Motion carried.

The contact list is also strewn with names that have lain dormant for years, either since the individuals concerned played a few games in the distant past or since they were suggested as possible recruitments— but which no one feels like removing because it's better for morale to look at a long list than a short list, or because they are handy as aliases for unregistered players, prison escapees, etc.

'Trevaskis?' asks Pete Macca. 'Anybody heard of him? Actually, we've got two of them. Must be brothers.' His imagination has been captured: for the rest of the evening, he advances the claims of this enigmatic coupling at every opportunity. Need another quick in the Thirds? 'Trevaskis.' Numbers four and five in the Fourths? 'The Trevaskises will enjoy playing together. And one can give the other a lift.'

To an eavesdropper it sounds like a murky business. 'Pockets replaces Malkovitch.' 'If we get Wasim, Panther can fill in for the Chef.' Codenames also evolve during the evening. Two new boys whom Big John has brought to training from a restaurant called The Keg become, inevitably, Trav Keg and Stewy Keg.* We also discuss a new finger-spinner, introduced by One Dad as 'Anthony from the Wine Shop', who, as no one has caught his surname, becomes 'A. Wineshop'.

Having not been seen to bat, Wineshop's place in the order is similarly speculative. 'I heard him say that he bowls a bit and bats a bit,' says Churchyard. Presto! Another all-rounder. If Wineshop continues advancing at this rate, the club presidency will soon be within his grasp.

Churchyard gives an impressive performance. He's canvassed for the Fourths job, and immediately set out to contract a core of players by ringing round the contact list—no doubt encountering a few ex-wives and

---

* The immediately associative nickname is a Yarras tradition. In 2000–1, we had the services of two boys from the Danish national squad. As nobody could pronounce their second names, they became Soren Denmark and Henrik Denmark. We miss them, and they miss us, as we found them jobs working behind a bar in a strip club.

ordering a few takeaways in the process. But he'll have his work cut out.

The choice of the Yarras Fourth XI has traditionally been a permanent work in progress, with a seemingly irreducible proportion of vacancies. For a time, as chairman of selectors, I used to fill the empty spaces with provisional scribblings like 'Bradman, D.' and 'Trumper, V.'; it certainly gave teams a stronger look. I then evolved one of our more enduring selection traditions—the cult of 'P. Harris'.

Pete Harris was a left-arm quick at the Yarras for many years, Doc's vice-captain in the Thirds, before becoming a physiotherapist in Cairns. As usual, though, he remained on the contact list, and I customised his name as a synonym for 'TBA'. Sometimes, selection meetings would end with the Fourths, the last team picked, containing 'P. Harris' four or five times; in other words, it was time to press-gang some fill-ins.

If a hole remained, a player from another team would have to double up at weekends and play as 'P. Harris'. Teammates would be instructed to refer to him as 'Harro', and the club statistican would be left to decrypt his identity for the end of season averages.

This sometimes proved impossible—either no one could remember or someone wanted to forget—and a residue of unclaimed runs, wickets and catches accrued. Luckily, 'P. Harris' has never quite won a trophy, otherwise a dozen or more players might lay claim to it.

The real 'Harro', who as part of the Yarras diaspora remains in contact with the club, loves the fact that his career record has continued to swell without direct involvement. Or he did until he rang for a yarn a few months ago, and said he was looking forward to coming back to Melbourne in a few years and rejoining the club. 'Sorry, mate,' I told him. 'You'll have to play under an assumed name.' He'll get used to being called Trevaskis.

Week 4

Bonding

Exploring South Yarra Cricket Club's history last year, we discovered that its origins lay more than a century ago in a social club for local gentry, whose keener cricketers had at some stage peeled away from various egg-and-spoon and tug-o-war factions.

This awareness, of course, detained us roughly half a minute. Obviously, much had changed: local gentry are as conspicuous at the Yarras as they are in the cast of 'Neighbours'. Yet the club as a pretext for innocent amusement survives: functions small and large festoon the calendar, commencing with a pre-season get-together just ahead of Round One.

When I joined the club nine years ago, the tradition was a Friday evening of discount drinks at a city nightclub, although this lost favour when the hostelry in question made Fridays its Goth night. One of the few sights than can prise a half-pissed Aussie from a bar is a teenage Marilyn Manson look-alike.

In 2000, the venue shifted to a pub, which may have succeeded had the committee not scheduled it for the night of the Olympic opening ceremony. Panther's recent advocacy of a club Brownlow night was sustained on the grounds that it would draw more than the previous year's six.

The Brownlow Medal is the Australian Football League's annual award to its best player. The votes are read aloud by the league's CEO, rather like a bingo call, but delivered with the gravity of a declaration of war. The audience is composed of footballers, genial thugs in tuxedos trying to look both coy and sober; alongside them lounge anorexic bottle-blondes. No night on television is so buttock-clenchingly embarrassing: imagine a music-free Eurovision Song Contest staged before several hundred nightclub bouncers.

The Yarras' efforts to savour this annual rite, however, were beset with difficulties. We hadn't received our club-room keys from the council, requiring us to grovel to the footy club ('You look like the grovelling type, Chairman.'). We have a television there so tiny that it would have been like watching the event through the wrong end of a telescope, demanding that we hustle up adequate equipment ('How old's your VCR mate?' 'Eh?'). And we had no beer; in fact, we had no beer twice, as the first supply was stolen from the back of Bourkey's ute. Panther e-mailed me rather desperately. 'Mate, this is looking like a debarcle.' Only his spelling could be disputed.

Overcoming these obstacles then left another: nobody had a clue how to connect the video projector, borrowed from one clubman, to the video recorder borrowed from another. For two hours prior to show-time, a group of grown men stood around thousands of dollars worth of recalcitrant machinery, hopefully plugging in wires and reading aloud from instruction manuals in the slow, deliberate and penetrating tones that tourists adopt with locals who don't speak English.

There was a false dawn when the projector suddenly detected a signal; panic resumed when it emerged that we could receive every channel save that on which the Brownlow was being telecast. Finally, Bourkey volunteered to fetch his television, Pete

Macca his portable antenna, and Moof and I the take-away pizzas.

Superficially, the evening had been a standard Yarras stuff-up. As the pizza pilgrims set forth on a windswept Monday night, we were catering for only twelve. Plans for running a Brownlow book had been abandoned, the names instead being distributed at random with first prize being the change from the pizzas. Yet strangely, an atmosphere of barely contained hilarity prevailed. Panther was glowing. Six last year, twelve this year: by his reckoning, we were way ahead.

The Brownlow provided the usual rich entertainment. Favourites were evaluated with vigour, blondes with appreciation. Disputes about the latter were resolved with that timeless Australian laconicism: 'Well, she's better-looking than my right hand.' The pool table was erected for an impromptu tournament, the uneaten food cheerfully thrown at one another, and by 1 a.m. everyone agreed that Manchester United and the New York Yankees weren't in it: the Yarras was the greatest sporting institution in the universe.

I struggle to explain now—the euphoria of my winning the pizza change aside—why the logic of this was so inescapable at the time. But there is something you derive from being the member of a sporting club, however humble, that is unobtainable from merely supporting a sporting club, however good.

Everyone has at some stage lived in a communal house, with all that this entails: rules, rosters, bad times, good times, Post-It notes on the yoghurt, and the lid left off the toothpaste. A good sports club is like the living room of the best shared household you ever lived in, where one's successes are everyone's, and one's disasters only add to the fund of stories told about one another. Then you can go home, and the lid is either on or off the toothpaste, just as you please. The local gentry a hundred years ago were onto something.

Week 5

Rain

The first day of our season in the Yarras Fourth XI, and Two Dads is disgruntled. 'I gave up breakfast with my wife and the possibility of a root to play today,' he complains. I could see his point.

The commencement of suburban cricket competition has coincided with Melbourne's traditional Indian winter. Birds bathe cheerfully in the bare patches on our outfield excavated by the local Aussie Rules club. I've pondered the possibility of off-spin in mittens. Interludes of play have been shrouded by drizzle, darkness and the fumes of burning martyr.

Two Dads* is bowling gamely. But running up into

---

* Two Dads' nickname sounds American Indian, something like Young Man Afraid of His Horse or Old Codger Who No Longer Hooks the Bouncer, but it pertains to his hyphenated surname,

a freezing gale, he's hitting the bat as hard as a meringue. To jolly him along, I inquire what sex with his wife is worth exactly. He muses: 'Five-for.' A big statement; perhaps this includes breakfast.

There's no opportunity for clarification. Soon after, Two Dads takes a step toward conjugal contentment by spectacularly crocking himself. Slipping as he drops a catch, he pulls a hamstring. Falling down, he strains a quadricep. The boundary rope looks like a veritable death trap as he limps off, but he manages to avoid tripping over it. See you after Christmas, mate.

Frankly, none of us seriously expected to play at all on this opening day given the abundance of rain the week before. Setting off in a hurry I've failed to pack my thigh pad, but in rifling my kit at the ground discover, *inter alia*, a six-month-old issue of the *Economist*, a fat book on the Battle of Jutland, a theatre ticket from May 1999, and a guide to feline oral hygiene. Either I took Trumper the cat to the vet at some stage on the way to training last season, or Trumper

---

Campbell-Burns. With the twisted logic so endemic at the Yarras, this means that another player whose surname is Campbell is nicknamed One Dad.

cunningly secreted it there herself, confident that I'd never find it.

We look, accordingly, very rusty, not to say crusty. Big John's first over for the season includes a full toss metres above the batsman's head, and a triple bouncer that zeroes in on point. I wear one in the chest when I get into position to hook, then remember I don't hook. 'Jeez, you're tough,' comments Tommy, my partner. 'No,' I confide. 'Just crap.'

The outcome might have been different had we been able to feel our extremities and hold our catches, although this is a bit like saying that Field-Marshal von Paulus had a fairly good war except for that muddle at Stalingrad. Fielding is always the faculty that returns last after inactivity, largely through apathy. To paraphrase Kenneth Tynan, we've been working on our fielding non-start for the last two months.

It is a grim beginning to the season. Our Firsts and Seconds are washed away, our Thirds cut short in a winning position. Rain. Okay, it's good for the lawn. Yes, it's nice for the farmers. And if you're a bachelor like me, it's handy for the washing up, if you get the plates outside quickly enough. But, at heart, we don't even like fictional rain in this country. How often does it really bucket down on 'Neighbours' or 'The Secret Life of Us'? And if it did, the programs would need to bear the prefatory notice: 'Caution. The following program contains scenes that may be distressing to some cricketers.'

At the Yarras, bad weather entails a lot of hanging round at the club rooms, cheating at pool, trying to light barbecues with copies of the club newsletter, and bragging about runs and wickets we haven't yet made or taken. Fortunately, we're blessed with a home ground whose grandeur is somewhat out of kilter with the standard of cricket it usually hosts. Como Park—carved from a hillside, hugged by the Yarra River, and overlooked by a heritage-listed colonial mansion—is reckoned among Melbourne's loveliest. Not least by us.

The club rooms, likewise, are disproportionately splendid: a rambling two-storey brick pavilion with a balcony for throwing parties on and hurling profanities off. Thanks to Bourkey, our Fourths keeper-cum-bar manager, it has a new couch and some rather fetching cafe-style umbrellas—my impression is that they sort of fell off the back of one truck onto the back of his.

But there are only so many beers and pies you can consume even in Australia. And some of us, like Two Dads, have homes and wives and families. That's a worry. If this rain continues there's a serious danger we might remember them.

Week 6

AB

A stirring address from Churchyard. 'Let's move on from last week, fellas,' he lectures the Yarras Fourth XI, rousing them for Round Two. 'We've gotta forget about it, and learn from the experience. This week, let's go one better and win.'

I was still ruminating on the internal logic of this as we took the field. If we forgot the first game, could we still learn from it? And if we remembered the first game, might the lesson be that it was better to have forgotten it?

Could we perhaps learn from the experience *then* forget? Or would the lessons seem less valid when detached from their origins? Is winning, furthermore, actually one better than losing? Surely it's two or three; it could be five the way we'd played in Round One. No wonder I've never gotten anywhere in this bloody game, dammit: when I should have been concentrating on keeping my left elbow up, I've been busily parsing syllogisms.

Luckily, my teammates ingest the rhetoric, and we improve by a solid single digit in comfortably rolling Brighton East. After an inauspicious fielding warm-up where we were convincingly outperformed by Jed, Wock's dingo cross, we caught with mercurial brilliance, and perpetrated three run-outs—as astounding to us as to our opponents. Modesty forbids disclosure of who was involved in two of them.

Perhaps there was another motive force, too. Pre-match ceremonies also included the unfurling of a banner honouring last season's Fourths' skipper, Churchyard's predecessor. Had I been writing this a year ago, AB would have been among the chief *dramatis personae*. He was a uniquely endearing character, sardonic and softly spoken, wise beyond his years, and capable of obtaining one's complete allegiance without ever seeking it.

AB had a mischievous sense of humour and a strong sense of the absurd; he once picked up a

German hitchhiker on the way to a game, and endeavoured to persuade him that he was a natural number five who bowled a bit. He was probably the most relaxed skipper I've ever known, to the extent he sometimes omitted to delegate a batting order when going out to open and left the team to sort it out themselves.

Over three years, I got to know AB well. We played indoor cricket in winter and dozed through numberless committee meetings in summer, even performed as a duet at the Yarras' karaoke night. I'd also often meet him—usually late, regularly hungover—prowling Balaclava station en route to work as a senior policy adviser at the Environment Protection Authority, and cutting an insouciant figure in dark suit, dark glasses and dark ponytail. We also tooled around in his gunmetal grey sports coupe, which AB justified on the basis that the front seat was big enough for a blonde and the boot big enough for the club kit.

It was behind the wheel of that car that AB died in May, aged thirty-one—decidedly the darkest day of my Yarras years, and that goes for us all. Fifty players from near and far attended AB's funeral—even the original 'P. Harris'—and we've looked since for ways to honour his memory. Big John has sponsored a Yarras one-day cap bearing the legend 'AB 1969–2001', I've dedicated a book to AB as 'a friend and example', and Squadron Leader's lavish banner will enjoy an honoured place among our *lares et penates*. It involves a range of AB action photographs, including a couple of him being run out by partner Womble—itself a classic Como experience.

I've long been leery of sports stars dedicating this and that performance to the Queen Mum or Kurt Cobain or their sick hamster. Does it mean they're unmotivated at other times? Or are they trying to convince us that the money doesn't matter, and that they reside in Monaco out of sheer reverence for the antiquity of the house of Grimaldi rather than the desire to be buried with their first dollar?

Yet I confess I feel a mite more strongly about this season than others. I've agreed to be 'contracted' to the Fourths, for all the good that might do them, and have been wearing AB's pads, for all the good that might do me. AB's father Ron donated his son's gear to the Yarras, and it now composes most of the Fourths' kit that rattles round in the rear of Churchyard's hatchback.

Lbws are still a bit of a hardship, but AB's partial involvement in the process of being dismissed enables me to be a bit more philosophical.

Churchyard is a quite different skipper to AB. He's very organised, very disciplined, and as disposed to earnest pep talks and rallying cries as AB was averse to them. He's a fine batsman and a smart guy, a consultant in civilian life with an undergraduate degree in psychology; indeed, I sometimes suspect him of doing fieldwork for a Skinnerian critique of middle-order collapses. But if we win a flag, I'll cheerfully referee the PhD.

Week 7

Practice

'You're dead, pal.'

'That's plumb. Tell your story walkin', mate.'

'You're a disgrace to the brothel your mother worked in.'

'If I want shit from you, I'll squeeze your head.'

It's an Aussie tradition, an indivisible part of our cricket heritage. Some would call it unacceptable, others a blight on the game's fair name. At the Yarras, we call it 'practice'.

Groucho Marx once said that no one is ever entirely displeased by the failure of their best friend, and I catch his drift when I knock someone over at a Yarras training session on Tuesday or Thursday evening, or am knocked over. Opponents you only see once.

Rivalries with clubmates can be sustained for years.

Rain having relented, we finally have our three outdoor turf practice pitches at Como Park in operation. And their operation always begins in the same fashion: we stand around asking each other who has the keys to open the equipment bunker in which we keep our nets, poles and pegs.

I once suggested that the Yarras adopt the motto *Noli me rogare ubi sint claves* ('Don't ask me where the keys are')—on the grounds that this was one of the most frequently heard phrases round the club, and that it sounded so much better in Latin. Broadly, the policy is that each captain gets a set of keys, because they need to open the rooms on match days. Womble also retains a set, because he would no sooner skip training than leave an uneaten snag on the barbecue.

It's up to Womble, then, to conceive of a system for transferring the keys on the occasions when he might be late to practice, and these are unfailingly Womblesque. 'What I'll do,' he explained to me once, 'is I'll give you the club-room keys now. That way you can get into the bar, and get the storeroom keys out of the drawer. And I'll put the bunker keys in the storeroom at the bottom of the shirtbox, with the fridge keys in case anyone wants a drink.'

I had to think about this. 'I don't get it. Why not simply give me the bunker keys now?'

But Womble looked so crestfallen—as though I'd somehow spoiled the game—that I just went along with it.

When the keys have been located, there's further standing round, as we try to remember how we last erected the nets. For putting up nets is one of those activities at which no one ever seems to improve (like, in my case, bowling off-spin). That's because it's not interesting enough to bother studying and...hell, they've only gotta stay up a few hours anyway.

Two universal laws govern net erection: a different approach must be used each time, and the more people involved the slower the process. A third can also come into play, which is that your troubles may not end when you get the nets up. No sooner had we stood back last season to admire one particularly baroque arrangement of tilting poles and extra string than a hairy brown mutt freed from its owner's lead barrelled in and levelled it.

At last, competition commences. This can mean as much time spent bickering as batting and bowling:

whether a snick might have carried, whether the bowler warranted a second slip, whether the umpire was competent to give an lbw. For a slow bowler like me, debate usually centres on the specifications of the 'virtual' ground. In my own mind, I am always bowling at the MCG; most of our batsmen seem to imagine themselves in a table-top 'Test Match' game. I've found that it also helps to pre-empt discussion with one or more stock abbreviations, like 'GSFNR' ('good-shot-for-no-runs') or 'MV' ('moral victory'). Otherwise the simultaneous cries—'Six!' from the batsman, 'Caught!' from me—can cause confusion.

From a distance, it is not the most eye-catching cricket spectacle. Wasim, a stockbroker, always turns up in a smart rig and what looks like brand new gear to go with his year-round tan (hence the nickname). But Easty, a house painter, is inclined to arrive from work in pants that he seems to have borrowed from Jackson Pollock. His equipment, likewise, is of improbable vintage. When Easty's flat was burgled recently and the thieves found his cricket bag, they tipped his gear on the floor and took the bag.

What practice *is*, though, is loud. There are appeals, send-offs, cries of exasperation, leers of triumph.

There's the noise of Castaway, our hippy fast bowler, thundering up to bowl in his Blundstones, which sounds like a stampede of brumbies. There's the racket of Womble ordering everyone round at the top of his voice, and commandeering twenty-minute batting sessions for himself in which every ball will be smeared in the direction of mid-wicket. It's always good to bat at the same time as Womble because a) you get twenty minutes, and b) you don't have to watch him bat.

Mind you, practice these days is a little gentler than in days of yore when we stretched a single net across the middle of the centre wicket—a rude improvisation permitting two players, back-to-back, to bat simultaneously. A flaw in this configuration was what became known as 'the Como ridge', the built-up earth on each surface normally occupied by the bowlers' creases. Hitting the right spot turned the most mundane medium-pacer into a bowler of Thommo-like lift. Denny, a Yarras stalwart, recalls a practice a week before a grand final for which he'd had the misfortune to be selected—misfortune because he edged out a quick bowler known, without ambiguity, as Bloodbath.

Bloodbath had one of those tightly coiled personalities, which in America would result in a cellar full of semi-automatic weapons and a library of millenarian prophecies. The light was dimming at about 8 p.m. when Denny took his knock that night, and the only intimation he had of the first delivery was a faint brush on his chin and Bloodbath's basilisk stare from a yard away. 'You're weak as piss,' Bloodbath snarled.

In the next ten minutes, Denny scarcely used his bat; Bloodbath had chosen a two-piece ball black with age and undetectable in the dusk. Later, in time-honoured Aussie fashion, Bloodbath bought Denny a beer. 'Just wanted to toughen you up for the final,' he explained.

'I'm looking forward to playing the West Indies now,' Denny replied.

Psychopaths aren't encouraged at the Yarras these days—or they're promoted to the committee, where they can't do much harm. And Bloodbath is now a mellower man with a couple of kids—the Bloodpuddles. But the competitive element to practice survives, even in fielding, where we have drills with euphonious names like Sudden Death, Last Man Standing and King.

King is a slips routine with a chucker and nicker.

Participants form a cordon. Catch one, and you remain where you are. Drop one, and you retire to the end of the line, gully or backward point, while everyone else advances one position. The object of the exercise is to negotiate your way to first slip—the regent of the routine's title.

It quickly occurred to me that the way to prosper in King was to score a quiet recess like fourth slip, and wait for those defending the top positions to err. Indeed, I've proposed it be renamed Bureaucracy, on the basis that you're unrewarded for doing the right thing, promoted only when superiors do the wrong thing, and that clawing your way to the top is futile: one mistake and you're busted to the ranks amid a chorus of derision. If the ousted King received a handsome pay-out, it would be the perfect metaphor for public service life.

Perhaps, though, that would contradict the ethos of practice. It isn't work; its lack of inhibition depends on its absence of significance. Thus Philip Hodgins's lines in his poem 'The Practice Nets':

> It doesn't matter how many times you're out
> You always carry your bat. It's like a dream.

And if you can't talk a good game…well, then you might have to play one.

Week 8

Mates

Cricket abounds in memorable partnerships. England had Hobbs and Sutcliffe, Australia Miller and Lindwall, New Zealand Reid and Wright (not a famous pairing but they should have been). The Yarras have their equivalent: Moof and Womble.

Moof is a gifted all-rounder who plays in our Firsts. He hurls himself into cricket with utter abandon, charging in to bowl fast with a face of screwed-up intensity, and regarding anything less than six to get off the mark as paltry. A mid-pitch conference with Moof is invariably a series of grunts about the virtues of prudence. 'C'mon chairman. Play each ball on its merits, and let's be here at the end. No reckless shots.' When you reply that your reckfulness can be taken as read, he'll confide: 'I know, I know. I'm talking to myself.'

Moof's cricket is an index of his unfailing gusto. He is crazily game for really stupid things—batting without a box, bowling left-handed, dangling from balconies by a hand, shaving his head and dyeing his scalp purple. He is also an irresistible raconteur, most stories beginning with the preamble 'I did this really stupid thing once...'

Above all, Moof has cult status at the Yarras for being the only guy we know who leaves a slipstream as he eats. It was said of batting with Bradman that he turned teammates into spectators. Dining with Moof is a similar experience. You eat. He eats. You stop. He continues. And continues. It's the gustatory equivalent of your partner taking a single off the last ball of every over. Moof recently failed to finish a can of spaghetti, and thought perhaps he was poorly until he read the label 'Serves Eight'. When I once asked him his life's ambition, thinking it might be of centuries or premierships, he replied without hesitation, 'To be locked in McDonald's after everyone's gone home.'

Nor is Moof's renown as trencherman confined to the Yarras. We were out a few months ago when Moof ordered some takeaway pizzas, which we then drove to collect. But when I popped in to do the necessaries at the relevant Toorak Road taverna, the lads behind the counter looked suspicious. 'Where is Moof?' they said. 'You will get Moof.'

It sounded serious, like a summons from Don Corleone. As soon as Moof walked in, though, everyone was wreathed in smiles: he was greeted like a popular benefactor, which it emerged that over the years he has been. Moof scattered his 'g'days' by name, inquired after wives and girlfriends and pets, and we departed with armfuls of pizzas, half of them freebies. A pizza box in Moof's custody must be like a bat in Steve Waugh's: the premium endorsement.

Womble, who plays with me in the Fourths, is a cricketer of altogether humbler attainments. He is a wide man who wields a 3lb bat, usually in the direction of cow corner, toddles between wickets like a stout commuter hastening to catch his bus, and who doesn't so much chase the ball as chaperone it to the boundary.

Womble is revered, however, as a club man of uncompromising fanaticism, up for all the dullest duties: restocking the bar, pampering the pitch, stop-watching batsmen at practice, talking to the associations, talking to the curator, talking to umpires...in fact, talking to anyone who'll listen. Conversation with him is like walking into the middle of a sentence which, in my case, has continued nine years with no sign of ending. 'I've got to pick up the new hessian on Monday. What's hessian made from? There's the new TR7. It's not as good as the TR6. Why are they digging those holes? Look at her; she's cute. Women, eh?' None of these remarks require an answer; it's simply that, for Womble, speech is as unconscious an act as respiration.

Womble was actually my first captain at the Yarras. He was impossible. Later he played under my captaincy. He was even more impossible. I condoned his habit of moving the field when my back was turned, until he directed me from cover to square leg. 'Fair go, Womble,' I complained. 'Respect the office if not the man.'

Womble is also inclined to drive you quietly crazy at practice, with stroke after stroke of intolerable ugliness played in utter po-faced seriousness. Once as he waddled in for his net, I remonstrated with him. 'Bloody hell, Womble. Bowling to you for practice is useless. Nobody in the world bats anything like you.' Womble's retort reflected his unshakeable self-confidence: 'All great batsmen are unique.' *Touché.*

All this should make Womble the teammate from hell. Yet there was a season where he was missing from Como Park because of work commitments. It was soooo quiet. You heard the wind in the trees, the enchanting birdsong. But wind and birds were bugger all help with covers, didn't have credit cards to buy grog for the fridge, wouldn't organise indoor net sessions on a Sunday, and couldn't give me a lift there either. So I love him like a brother—brothers, of course, having a capacity for annoying the bejesus out of you.

There wouldn't seem to be much in common between Moof and Womble, but—cricket being a funny game—they are sincerely, solidly, mates. They banter away like an old married couple, treat the club rooms as their pied-a-terre in summer, and play footy together at Como Park in winter. 'Womble's very courageous,' Moof says. 'You've just got to slow the game down till he gets there.' I can't conceive of the Yarras without them. I guess there would be more for everyone to eat. But there'd be less of everything else.

The Yarras: A User's Manual

Last summer at training, I asked Easty if I could borrow his gear. It was, as ever, a shambles. 'How is it,' I asked, 'that you've ended up with one velcro pad and one with a strap and buckle?'

'It's a symbol of the fact that we're an evolving club,' he replied.

Evolving? I guess that's one way to describe it. Perhaps I should pause here to address some OAQs—Occasionally Asked Questions—about how a cricket club like ours functions at the dawn of the twenty-first century.

The Yarras are an incorporated association. This emerged when we discovered our constitution lying in a drawer behind the bar three years ago. Our then-secretary CC, like Malcolm Turnbull, proposed a phase of constitutional reform. We put the constitution in a different drawer and, also like Malcolm Turnbull, he quickly lost interest.

The Yarras annual general meeting is held around Juneish-Julyish-Augustish. Failing that, in September. Or October. November at the latest. As it's usually at the pub owned by CC's missus, it's best to get the serious stuff out of the way in the first half-hour to allow three or four hours of free-form business without notice. This is usually dominated by Moof, Womble or Castaway (if he's had a few cones).

The Yarras annual meeting elects the Yarras committee. That is, there are usually seven or eight guys who fail to rule themselves out either because a) they're new, b) they're naively of the belief that it can't be as bad as last season, or c) they're not there. In the a) category for 2001–2 are Kreuger, Bourkey and Panther; in the b) are TB, Womble, McFly, Fat Tony and myself; in c) is Mulva, the club secretary—has there ever been a costlier trip to Bali?

There are exceptions. Sometimes efforts are even made to persuade suitable people to serve on the committee, and a good time to hit on them is when you've just done them a favour. Womble and I recently gave Rasputin a lift home from training for this express purpose. Rasputin is a social worker, which we guessed would make him a soft touch.

'Much as I'd like to, fellas,' he said, 'I think I'll be too busy. I've just joined the committee for a voluntary organisation providing assisted accommodation to schizophrenics.'

'But that's good!' suggested Womble. 'You'll bring committee experience.'

'That's not the only experience you'll bring,' I added.

'Mysteriously,' said Rasputin, 'I'm expecting to have my work phone, home phone and e-mail all cut off indefinitely.'

'But we know where you live now!' Womble protested.

'No you don't,' Rasputin replied. 'See that manhole cover over there? I actually live in the sewers.' It's so much easier to elect people who don't show up.

The Yarras committee convenes monthly, either round TB's kitchen table or at the club rooms. TB (president) gives us a rev. Mulva (secretary) advises on incoming correspondence, which often includes something dotty from the council, like an inquiry as to why we don't have a written policy on hats. Fat Tony (treasurer) complains about increasing costs, such as increased premiums since our insurer decided we needed protection from Taliban attack. Womble (delegate) distributes stuff from the last association meeting he attended, such as a discussion paper concerned with the covering of wickets on days of the week with an r in them. McFly (sponsorship liaison) will advise that the last twenty companies he contacted about sponsorship all told him to bugger off, but that he's undismayed: 'I'm used to having my face slapped.' Panther (social secretary) will report on upcoming social events, and open for debate issues of operational nitty-gritty. At the last meeting the issue was how much grog to order for karaoke night. Mulva: 'Some chicks might want a few softies.'

Kreuger: 'Not on my table, mate.'

The Yarras committee also appoints the captains. In 2001–2, this means Pete Macca (Firsts), Dave Macca (Seconds), Doc (Thirds) and Churchyard (Fourths), who with me constitute the selection panel. This is my last year as chairman. I *mean* it this time.

All deliberations are passed on to players through

three main conduits:

The website. Distribution of important information. Maintained by Pete and Dave Macca. Have a look. The address: yarras.com. Yes, we really exist. Gosh. Just like 'Big Brother', isn't it?

The e-mail list. Distribution of jokes. Maintained by everybody. Sorry, you can't look at this. Some proprieties must be maintained.

The newsletter. Distribution of important information masquerading as jokes, and vice versa. Maintained by me. It's called the *South Yarra Sentinel*. It is fifteen to twenty pages a month of gossip, in-jokes and libel, run off on my publishers' photocopier when they're not looking, and stapled together on my kitchen bench. You could look at this, but as an outsider would find it wholly incomprehensible.

Impressive, eh? Particularly impressive, I think, for a club that still has gloves in its kit with green rubber spikes on them. There's more, too. Posterity received a boost last summer when our Pete Macca—either an unemployed bum or a professional punter, depending on the day's luck—compiled 190. This may or may not have been the club's highest score. Reference books—for me *Wisden*, for Pete the form guide—were strangely silent on the subject.

Pete, a computer boffin whenever he strays into the workforce, took the initiative. He and Dave spent winter designing a web-based record-keeping system, ResultsVault, keying-in dozens of old scorebooks; these were in varying states of decay, stained with bits of afternoon tea and emitting an odour of unwashed socks, having reposed for years in the bottoms of captains' bags. With a few keystrokes, you can now look at your Yarras career figures (so I'm told). Amazing.

Hmmm. I've almost convinced myself. Maybe we *are* an evolving club. Now there's just the question of what we'll evolve into.

Week 9

Names

Devotees of sporting cliche will be familiar with the phrase 'a great side on paper'. Its definition is subtly different at the Yarras: for us, a 'great side on paper' has meant eleven names plus a few phone numbers should anyone go fishing or suffer a twinge in their punting muscles on Saturday morning. But times are changing.

It didn't happen all at once. At one early selection meeting, Pete Macca proposed that numbers ten and eleven in the Seconds be occupied by 'Ian, Josh's mate' and 'Justin, Josh's mate Ian's mate', on the basis of a fleeting appearance at training by the former, and rumour of the latter.

On the receiving end, Dave Macca looked suspicious. 'So what does Ian do?' he asked. 'Bowls medium pace,' replied his brother, an assessment based firmly on imagination. 'And Justin's very talented. Could be anything.' It was like watching one brother try to convince the other that the raygun he wanted to play with wasn't that cool, and that the Play-Doh was much better.

Neither IJM nor JJMIM was available to play, as it happened, and neither was heard of again. For reasons little understood, however, new players continue to rock up weekly: talented young players, too, shaving about ten years off the average age.

For the first time in memory last week, we adjourned a selection meeting without needing to call anyone. More players were available than places. Reading the teams was an emotional moment. I fleetingly imagined myself a real chairman of selectors, rather than a glorified paging service. I fantasised of counselling my colts: 'If you want to scale the giddy heights, boys, you'll have to make sacrifices. Fast women and slow horses have nipped many a career in the bud. As the Don once said to me—yeah, we were old mates—"Cricket is about respect. R-E-S-T-E-C-P. Especially for my bitches."' Fair dinkum. The Don never missed 'Ali G'.

Assimilating this new playing talent has imposed strains financial, social and cultural. And one important implication required prompt attention—we faced an acute shortage of nicknames. That selection evening at a nearby pizza joint, an ad hoc sub-committee for nomenclature was constituted: Moof, Womble and Tragic (that's—how shall I put this?—me).

Nicknames matter. A name merely reflects your parents' tastes. A good nickname reflects an aspect of the way you are now, Moof and Womble being cases in point. Moof's handle began as a play on his surname, but fits his goofy gusto. Womble not only resembles one in physique, but in the garrulous fussiness with which he cleans up after us (an added benefit is that, having never watched 'The Wombles', he has no idea what we're talking about). Tragic I'm not going to comment on. It's my book.

The ad hoc sub-committee ruminated on great Yarras institutions of the past. We recalled the likes of Twang (named for the loudness with which his hamstrings used to explode), Whispers (inspired by the sound of his baggy tracksuit pants as he ran in to bowl at practice), and Humphrey (for his soundless appeals). Then we set ourselves the target of sufficient new nicknames to cover my cigarette packet. It filled rapidly.

Some are unprintable. Some should probably remain etymologically obscure: Space Cadet, Normal, Penfold, Kodak, Tripod, Wonder Dog Two, Hot Dog, Chilli Dog—Moof and Womble were getting hungry by this time. For one club man the name Gunner was floated—he's always gunner do this and gunner do that. For another, the name Moo came up—apparently his wild and reckless days involved an unsavoury incident with a cow. Funny what you learn about teammates over a few beers. Wonder if his wife knows?

In other cases, we built on existing foundations. For the last couple of years we've had a very slippery hippy fast bowler who, thanks to his ponytail and luxuriant beard, has become known as Castaway, from the Tom Hanks film. His brother, new to the club, has now been baptised Wilson, after Hanks's only companion on his desert isle: this makes him the first player in Yarras history named after a volleyball.

Twenty new nicknames had been coined by the

close of proceedings. Some may stick, others may not, but a solid start had been made. While we may revert in time to our old definition of 'a great side on paper', Moof and Womble had helped select a very useful side on my cigarette packet.

Week 10

Customs

'It's tough out here,' confides Churchyard as I come out to join him at the weekend. True, the scenario doesn't look promising: from the vantage of our five for 50, the target of 110 appears gargantuan, especially as our tail has recently not so much wagged as writhed in agony.

Yet no, Churchyard informs me, the situation is still worse. 'The pitch is playing tricks. Some balls are exploding. Some are going along the ground. The guy you're facing is pretty sharp. Watch out for the one he seams away. He bowls an off-cutter too. The left-armer's bowling inswingers, but don't get hit on the pads: the umpy's completely clueless.'

I gulp. 'A simple "good luck" would have sufficed.'

Churchyard grins. 'Oh, don't pay any attention to me. I've only faced one ball so far.'

Another instance of Churchyard using his psychology degree? Actually, no. He is indulging in a time-honoured park cricket custom: the Partner's Perspective, a kind of greeting-cum-briefing from the surviving batsman to the newcomer. They aren't usually as elaborate and unmanning as Churchyard's—a pro-forma 'get forward' or 'loud calls' will suffice—but they can vary in depth and intensity.

A few seasons ago, Wasim greeted me with, 'You know what? I had a dream about us batting together last night.'

'Really?' I asked. 'How did I go?'

'You batted well,' he recalled.

I was immediately suspicious. 'Have you been taking a lot of drugs lately?'

'No really,' he assured me. 'You were smashing 'em everywhere.'

'You've got some serious issues, Waz. I suggest you see a psychiatrist.'*

The Partner's Perspective has been on my mind of

---

*As it was, we did bat a while that day, allowing me to tax Wasim between overs about how I'd been dismissed; being as superstitious as the next cricketer, I imagined eliminating that shot from my late, because I've lucked on a guide to such customs. Written in 1954, Lt-Colonel A. T. Burlton's *Cricketing Courtesy* was a kind of *Emily Post's Etiquette* for the flannelled fool, and heartily endorsed by E. W. Swanton, H. S. Altham and A. E. R. Gilligan—perhaps out of solidarity with another unfortunate whose parents had given him initials instead of full names.

Cricket Courtesy brims with old world civilities. Burlton counselled batsmen that, in the event of a streaky stroke, it was 'considered courteous to offer the bowler a word of apology'. He enjoined bowlers to 'avoid gesticulating or by some other method giving vent to your feelings because a ball just shaves the stumps'. And he reminded fielders that 'another of cricket's delightful habits is the applause by the fielding side for a six'.

The Yarras, it has to be said, didn't measure up frightfully well. I once saw Torqs, our most outspoken fast bowler, applaud a six off his bowling, but that was simultaneous with an inquiry about whether the batsman would be dying intestate or not. And when

---

repertoire. Sadly, he couldn't remember, or at least not until I mishit to cover. As I walked off, he commented excitedly, 'That was it!' Cue 'Twilight Zone' theme.

Churchyard recently 'walked' on 96, having been given not out for a catch at the wicket, the reaction was one of utter consternation.

'It would have been a shallow hundred,' he explained.

'Shallow hundred!' I exclaimed. 'Hey, give me a shallow hundred. I'm not proud.'

Dave Macca chimed in, 'Reckon I'd settle for a half-a-toe-dipped-quickly-in-a-puddle hundred.'

On the other hand, the park game is not devoid of courtesies. One appealing archaism is the Skipper's Salute. 'Opposition captain, boys!' the fielding skipper will announce as his rival takes guard, and a ripple of obedient applause ensues—sometimes followed by the audible advice to a fast bowler about making the innings as brief and bloody as possible.

Another nicety is the Post-Match Handshake, well-intended, though it can be hard to unclench your hand from a fist after a bad-tempered game. Many years ago, I played on mats with a bloke called Stoofer in a rancorous match where a gully fielder successfully claimed to have caught him on the bounce. I observed them aclasp afterwards, and expressed surprise. 'It's okay,' said Stoofer. 'I've just had a shit and there wasn't any paper.'

Many customs revolve around the rituals of drinks and afternoon tea. Drinks, for example, must last long enough for one cigarette, while tea, in our class of cricket the responsibility of the home team, should exclude everything with any pretensions to health or freshness.

The ideal tea, I've always thought, should be like dying and going to bachelor heaven, and the standard tea-time bill of fare at Como Park follows this description fairly accurately. Barbecue shapes are popular; likewise sticky buns, Tim Tams and corn chips. The ideal sporting diet, really—ideal for watching sport on TV, that is. And strictly speaking it could hardly be otherwise, cricket at the Yarras being about as close as you can get to life as a couch potato without having a remote control in your hand. Oh, and one other thing to remember if you're playing with us—you should always have at least started tea by the time Moof gets there. That's not so much a custom as advice.

At the Yarras, there's also the Away Beverage. Those returning to Como Park from an away fixture are entitled to one gratis drink chosen from our wide range of…well, of beer. There also used to be the institution of the Umpy's Beverage: a freebie for any official who'd stood at Como Park, although this is now restricted to those officials who've given fewer than six lbws.

Of course, I never expected Burlton's world to bear much relation to ours. His book, written many years before sledging, mentions only in passing the on-field yap that is now *de rigueur*. 'To get the reputation of "talking people out" is not a great compliment.' And it certainly never occurred to Burlton that the fella trying to talk you out might be your own partner.

Week 11

Stories

The Russian Fast Bowler. It might be a collaboration between John le Carré and Hugh de Selincourt. Or perhaps English cricket's latest saviour.

> Siberian superstar Izzy Gudenoff, who learned reverse swing by ballasting cricket balls with borscht but who is qualified for Derbyshire under a wrinkle in ICC rules, said yesterday he was gob-smacked to be picked for the Lord's Test. 'I am gob-smacked,' he declared (through an interpreter).

In fact, this is one of the more enduring Yarras clubroom yarns. It involves a bear-like fast bowler of

Russian extraction who some years ago became involved in a sledging duel with our former First XI captain. One side of the dialogue was in English, the other in an impenetrable guttural dialect sounding like Boris Yeltsin in his cups.

The denouement was the denial of an lbw appeal. The pacenik sprinted from the field, began head-butting a tree and contrived to render himself unconscious. The association took no action, commenting that everyone knew what fast bowlers are like.

Then there's The Guy Who Jumped in the River. This involves another opposition fast bowler—maybe the association was right, after all—who also adjourned a game in mid-over by bolting for the boundary and disappearing across the road that girdles our Como Park home, heedless of the heavy traffic.

The mystery wasn't solved until his sheepish return half an hour later, drenched, having hurled himself into the Yarra. A tube of Deep Heat had apparently leaked in his pocket, stimulating quite the wrong muscle.

Most nights at the Yarras, when memories are grog-jogged, a range of similar stories are guaranteed revival and retelling: The Day We Had a Streaker, The Team Who Had a Dog Fielding for Them, The Club

That Served Hash Cake at Afternoon Tea, plus others in the Giant Rat of Sumatra category (stories for which the world is not yet prepared).

A personal favourite is The Confused Umpire. This originated from a dialogue overheard at Royal Park, when an opposition batsman given out amid a flurry of bat, gloves and pads remonstrated belligerently with the presiding official. 'How the fuck was that out?' he demanded. 'Caught behind or lbw?' The umpire replied thoughtfully, 'A bit of both.'

At some point while these yarns are being repeated, there will be the inevitable interjection: 'You know, we really should write the club history.' All will agree that this is an Excellent Idea, and Something That Must Be Done—providing, of course, it entails no time, effort or cost.

It's a common dilemma. Most clubs have a sizeable stock of folklore. Most clubs leave it lodged in their members' heads. We're no different. We talk about 'the annals' of the Yarras, but little has been annalled; with burgers on the barbecue and beers in the fridge, nobody much fancies annalling.

With the boffo ResultsVault record-keeping system that Pete and Dave Macca have designed, however, we do now know a bit about our last thirty years. I could even check if I wished on how many times I've been lbw at the club (although I suspect this is better not to know).

The Yarras or something like them span more than a hundred years. Why, we even have our own Test cricketer. It dates back to South Yarra's days in the Southern District Cricket Association before World War I, when they were represented by one Donald Blackie, then in his early twenties and bound for glory. That a quarter of a century elapsed between his stints in the baggy blue and baggy green, and that he made his Test debut at the age of forty-six, scarcely weakens our sense of proprietorship. On the contrary, he is the *beau ideal* of the 'age-is-no-bar' school.

But, well, that history...does seem like a lot of work. Not much hope of getting Mr Blackie's co-operation either. Except by ouija board.

One day driving to practice, however, Pete Macca and I have a blinding flash—one unrelated to The Day We Had a Streaker. The problem with most club histories, we agree, is that they contain sentences like: 'During the 1911 annual meeting at the Mechanics' Institute, members unanimously approved the purchase of a new set of bails.' 'F. Bloggs received an electroplated cheese dish for his unbeaten 15 against the Flat Earth Society XI.'

'Every club's got a history with facts,' I mused. 'Why not become the first club with a history that's entirely made up?'

Pete is way ahead of me. 'You know, it's regrettable that historians have ignored W. G. Grace's many guest appearances with the Yarras,' he says. 'Especially the one where he claimed that the bails had been dislodged by the wicketkeeper's fart.'

So we're going with it: provisional deadline 2025, as we need to organise the karaoke night first. We'll tell the story of Don Bradman's war years, when he represented the Yarras incognito as Brad Donman; of the origin of Bodyline in the Yarras' ploy Waistline, which involved taking the piss out of overweight opponents; of Kerry Packer's plan of a WSC Yarras XI for his infamous circus, thwarted by the club's stance that night cricket *with* lights was 'for wimps'.

M. K. Gupta is bound to make several appearances: our flair for batting collapses must have some explanation. And Duncan Fletcher can forget about Izzy Gudenoff. He's our man now.

Week 12

Songs

Social functions at the Yarras can be hard to distinguish from the normal run of events, and the distinction is particularly fine in December. Broadly speaking, beer + barbecue + cricket = average day; beer + barbecue + singing = social function.

Saturday night is the Yarras end-of-year karaoke evening—Karaoke Khristmas at Komo, or KKK for short ('and,' the promotional flyer stated, 'we're not talking bedsheets with eyeholes'). The bottom line, of course, is that we need the money, and winkling wads out of wallets when people are pissed seems a more socially acceptable way of doing so than mugging them in the car park after training. But we also like a good time, and are no strangers to ritually humiliating ourselves: some of us do it every weekend.

It is, as usual, a very good night. Master of ceremonies Panther handles the job with confidence and aplomb, while judges Mrs Panther, Mrs Mulva and their friend Jo are either vicious but fair, or fair but vicious, depending on your standpoint. And having taken five catches for the Fourths that day, Normal is the ideal man to wield the Cymbals of Despair: our proxy gong.

Planning had not been without its hitches. On Tuesday, Panther and I had scouted the rooms to check the state of the amenities, furtively exploring the women's toilets—not nearly so much a wish fulfilment for men as is popularly believed, and certainly not in this instance.

'Jeez, what's that smell?' asked Panther. We traced it to one of the cubicles: the toilet had been very well used indeed.

'That's...errr...some stool,' observed Panther.

'It's almost a chair,' I said. 'Should we try and flush it?'

'Either that or shoot it.'

Panther took the first option, but the bullet might have been cheaper: the lavatory suddenly began to fill.

We stood back in silent horror as it brimmed to the rim of the bowl. Hanky the Christmas Poo, treading water on the surface, eyeballed us defiantly. 'Any other bright ideas, Panther?' I asked.

'Close the door, walk away, and use lots of Glen 20,' he said. But what might have been a crisis was averted by Mulva a few days later; performing a similar recce to ours, he fearlessly flushed the lavatory again, with more rewarding results. Panther and I exchanged guilty glances when he reported back. 'Thou hath slain the jabberwock, my son,' I told Mulva.

There are some last-minute absentees when the curtain goes up, with Churchyard finding the most original excuse. 'My ex-wife loved karaoke,' he explains. 'It totally freaks me out.' But, far from it being difficult to find volunteers on the evening, it proves almost impossible for Panther to arrest the tide of exhibitionism. Bloodbath is surprisingly coherent on 'Little Deuce Coupe', Pete Macca is coolly poised on 'Teddy Bear', and Moof utterly unstoppable in everything. Having clearly heeded his captain's injunction to build partnerships this season, he is keen to become involved in every song; in effect, each tune becomes a Moof Mix—i.e. the normal song and a drunken voice singing along, three octaves out of tune and several beats out of time.

'A solid performance,' purrs Panther unvaryingly after each one. 'A very solid performance.' It sounds like Alan Joyce on one of his less articulate days. What about that barbecue, Panther? 'Solid, mate, a solid performance.' And the attendance is good, eh? 'A very solid performance indeed.' 'Does he say that to you after sex?' Mrs Mulva asks Mrs Panther at one point; I keep to myself the possibility that Panther is harking back to what we'd found in the Ladies.

Winners for the evening are Pockets and Kreuger for their rendition of that vernacular folk classic 'Th'boislahdupp', each becoming entitled to half a sunhat—one half signed 'Greg', the other 'Chappell'—obtained by Panther through his South Aussie connections. But the evening becomes really interesting after 1 a.m.; with the competition complete and patrons either drifting away or falling asleep, freeform improvisation begins. Pete Macca, Castaway and Bourkey decide to attempt the entire Beatles Anthology.

They are still going four hours later, having just reached the 'Magical Mystery Tour' period, which I interpret as time to go. The sight of wheely bins overflowing with empties sets me in a cheerful mood, implying some relief of our overdraft. They are, of course, quite often full. But, as the song says, it ain't what you do, it's the way that you do it.

Opponents: A Survey

A few years ago, I began to be troubled by my decrepit gutters. They were adequate at collecting rain but tended to overflow, obscuring the house in a wall of water. The efficiency of the arrangement was of no concern, but passers-by might have mistaken it for an elaborate feng shui display.

I obtained a string of quotes which helped to clarify one issue: that I was ill-suited to dealing with the quotes once I'd obtained them. Then, totally confounded by company salesmen with glossy brochures and persuasive patter, I found a solo operator called John who offered to do the job more cheaply on the basis that he couldn't work past 3 p.m. on Tuesdays and Thursdays.

'How come?' I asked.

'Cricket practice,' he explained.

'You're hired.'

This isn't how they advise you to sift tradesmen on 'Better Homes & Gardens', of course, but I'm comfortable with it. On the whole, it's my naive belief that cricketers are a pretty decent bunch. There's the odd plonker, but they're mostly the ones who go on to be Australian prime minister. And it's worth reflecting that with even the craziest junkyard dog of an opponent, you have already, through cricket, a good deal in common.

In the Mercantile Cricket Association, of whose C-Grade the Yarras Fourths are members, opponents come in all shapes and sizes, with all manner of lore, customs and traditions. There's Burnley, a venerable club founded as a matting side in 1935; folklore has it that their first mats were delivered by bicycle from Melbourne's notorious Pentridge Prison. There's Gunbower, a one-team outfit named by its founders in 1973 after returning from a camping holiday near a country town called Gunbower on the Murray River. There's Reds, an outgrowing of the renowned Royal Park Reds formed in 1979 by members of the

Communist Party of Australia, the International Socialists and various fellow travellers, whose all-purpose sledge used to be 'hammer 'n' sickle 'em'.* Our strongest opponents at present are Powerhouse, a cricket and footy club with a robust culture: fielders at fault have to accept custody of a sunhat inscribed 'IFU' (I Fucked Up). Mind you, their knockabout crew don't take themselves too seriously either. Their captain Mike came in one day to the ritual welcome: 'Here's the skipper. He can't bat and he can't bowl.'

'Yes,' he retorted, 'but somebody's got to do the paperwork.'

The Yarras' favourite rivals, however, are Sacred Heart, brainchild of the eclectic Evo. My first knowledge of Evo was as a cagey seamer for Powerhouse. It turned out that he was a bit of a go-getter, though one for whom going and getting were of equal significance. In his early thirties, Evo is irrepressibly

---

* In the definitive historical overview of the Royal Park Reds in *Baggy Green*, vol. 1 no. 1, founding member and true believer Tony Roberts remarks that 'the political orientation of the average Reds cricketer has diluted from activist red to bohemian pink'. He recalls how an academic Marxist at mid-off would stir him to greater bowling efforts with cries of 'Praxis! Praxis!'

enthusiastic about all his undertakings, whether working as a fast-talking sportscaster on community radio, campaigning as an independent for local council, or fronting Australia's foremost Devo tribute band, Davo (to whom, having seen them thirty times, I am honorary groupie).

Three years ago, Evo decided he'd like his own cricket club, and founded it in association with St Kilda's Sacred Heart Mission, where he was a volunteer worker. The Hearters wear caps of Aboriginal red, black and gold, take turns wearing their one team blazer, and have equipped their Fawkner Park redoubt with a bar, fridge and turntable. Earlier this season I was an honoured guest at the turntable's official inauguration, plundering my vinyl collection to donate the first Jane's Addiction LP and *Cockney Rejects Greatest Hits Volume 3: Live and Loud*. Funny the things you can live without.

As this should make clear, competition between the Yarras and the Hearters, while keen, is hardly cutthroat. I've occasionally even filled in for the Hearters, hold social club membership No. 0102044, and enjoy their happy mix of accomplished cricketers and novices, such as Gavo, Davo's keyboard player, who, in his early forties, is learning to play cricket on the Internet. The Yarras had a terrific game against the Hearters this season where Gavo thwarted us with the deadest of bats, showing the benefit of all those Google searches for 'forward defensive stroke'.

Evo and his girlfriend Rosie have since been hosting a sports program on independent radio station 3RRR, 'Feelin' Kinda Sporty', between midnight and 2 a.m. on Fridays. I'm their slightly donnish co-host, punctuating the weightier ponderings of other guests (Evo's teammates Pumper, H, D-Rock and J-Lo) with rambling interpolations about the origins of the reverse sweep and such. It's community radio at its best: the first talkback caller was my mum, the second was Moof.

Mind you, a sporting rivalry, while it can be sporting, remains a rivalry. So it proved with John the gutter man, who it emerged not only played cricket, but did so for a club in the same competition as the Yarras. John took a while to execute his assignment on my roof, partly because every time he took a smoko, we'd subtly try pumping each other for information about our respective clubs: 'So, deck playing okay this season?' 'And this opening bowler of yours, how quick would you reckon he is?' 'Afternoon teas all right down your way?'

I think I came out ahead in this transaction because we later gave his boys a bit of a touch-up. That day it was 'G'day John', 'G'day Gideon', and nothing but 'Howzat' thereafter.

On the other hand, I may have to reconsider if the gutters start leaking this winter.

Week 13

Character

Cricket is allegedly a test of character, reintroducing its practitioners to triumph and disaster on a regular basis, while requiring them to treat those two impostors just the same. And having four XIs at the Yarras means that we can be treating them just the same at the same time.

This is turning out to be quite a good season. We're winning more often than losing, and almost everyone's been a contributor, either with bat, ball, or barbecue tongs. With a bit of luck, the Seconds will make the finals in their grade, while the Thirds and Fourths will have to test positive to a banned substance to miss out—unlikely, unless the prohibited list is widened to include VB.

It's just a pity about our Firsts. They haven't won a game this season and, like Kipling's Gentlemen-Rankers, 'are dropping down the ladder rung by rung'. This isn't for want of talented cricketers. Pete Macca and Pockets are quality batsmen, while Kinger and Humphrey are a first-rate new-ball pairing. With the all-round talents of Moof, there should be the basis of a handy side.

But something is clearly lacking, and there's no want of theories—or, at any rate, theories that might get us all off the hook. 'I've been thinking,' Pete Macca confided last week. 'It must be a leadership problem. Yeah, the captain has to take the rap. Reckon I should probably resign.'

'Hey, hang on a minute,' I protested. 'You're not resigning before I bloody well do. No, it's clearly a selection problem. I shall just have to fall on my Slazenger.'

'I've got to put my hand up here,' interrupted Mulva. 'My performance keeping the minutes at committee meetings has been disgraceful. I've decided to go before I'm pushed.'

By this time, we had been joined by club president TB, social secretary Panther, bar manager Bourkey and several members of the committee. Resignation? You beauty. An orgy of self-inculpation ensued. At the end of the evening, everyone had quit, the club had folded, and we were all about to take up gardening, devote weekends to our wives and children, and get more involved in the local community.

There was merely the question of what to do with all our gear. 'Jeez, I'd love a game of cricket,' I said. 'Fuck yeah,' said everybody else.

It's easier for us than for Pete Macca, who's not been in the pinkest form, and who is staring the club's Ducks Award in the face; so intently, in fact, that he e-mailed me to say that the duck he picked up in our practice match at Wangaratta would not count in official Yarras records.

Malcolm Speed clearly started something in the recent Test-that-wasn't-a-Test at Centurion Park. 'Yarras officials have expressed dissatisfaction with the fat pissed prick who was supposed to be match referee, but who was asleep in his own vomit,' Pete advised. 'The ICC has had no choice but to declare the match "unofficial" and has instructed statisticians to ignore it.' Pete speaks with authority, too, as he is the only guy at the Yarras who can be bothered keeping the stats.

In general, though, spirits are undepressed, and the effect on bar takings has been revenue neutral: while the Seconds, Thirds and Fourths have been celebrating, the Firsts seem to have been drowning their sorrows in roughly equal measure.

And sometimes losing makes a better story than winning. Even the Firsts' feat against Ajax of losing five wickets for one—a wide—took on spellbinding qualities at the clubroom the subsequent evening. Bourkey and Churchyard had blazed big scores in the Thirds and Fourths that day, but these were of lesser moment; the Firsts' scorebook was passed round with fascinated hilarity, its five fat ducks resembling a tortured revision of the Olympic symbol. Moof was told that the way he had let the wide go was a lesson for younger players.

It may be, in fact, that we're not quite depressed enough. There have been team meetings, reviews, previews and bonding sessions. But somehow, possibly thanks to Moof, all these have involved him eating copious quantities of pasta and tira misu at his favourite trattoria, Tamani's, while the rest of us talk about how Mark Waugh is finished and who our footy teams might pick up in the draft.

In any case, I'd rather it this way than the opposite. I've played in teams where it's been expected one would 'bleed for the club'. Bollocks to that. If I feel like bleeding, I'll visit the blood bank. And as for those impostors, well, I'm content in their company: I play with impostors every week.

Week 14

Injuries

A salient difference between English and Australian cricket, so it's said, is that the former is a full-time occupation, the latter a part-time preoccupation. At the Yarras, the distinction isn't so crisp. Sure, we play only either or both days of the weekend. But we then spend five days recovering.

As I compose this dispatch, my right knee is twice its normal size, propped on an upturned bin, and obtaining only minimal relief from a plastic bag of ice cubes: the result of an unruly bounce at our ground's Sahara End a couple of days ago. Como Park has two extremities: the Sahara End is traditionally a semi-arid zone, its sparse grass cover often causing the ball to take unpredictable deviations; and the Dogshit End, favoured for 'walkies' by the local doggie set, which also requires care, for different reasons.

When a furtive inspection revealed that I was growing a second knee cap, I sought the first-aid kit—i.e. Bourkey chipped a chunk of ice from the beer chiller, which I lashed to my leg with the tourniquet of a Yarras practice shirt. Sports medicos recommend RICE for bruising, which I think stands for Rest, Ice, Compress, Elevate. In my case it should stand for Retire, Immediately, Crippled, Enthusiast.

Bourkey himself is also *hors de combat* at present and has been anaesthetising himself with the non-ice contents of the beer chiller since snapping a bone in his hand while drilling into a block of concrete. For it's not only on the field that we risk indisposition—those pesky other lives of ours that interrupt the cricket week can be perilous, too.

Chef, who is an actual chef, suffers tendonitis in his bowling arm, because it is also his soup-stirring arm. Wogger and Apu, who work nightshift at the casino and in a service station respectively, often resemble men conducting personal experiments on the effects of sleep deprivation. Torqs, who doesn't need work to disturb an already erratic body clock, didn't quite make it to a recent game because of bites—those on the end of his fishing rod. Even one's personal life is dangerous at times. I almost missed a game a year ago when an ex-girlfriend stamped on my bare foot with her stiletto heel at 4 a.m. I managed to play only by borrowing an oversized boot and shortening my run-up to one hobble.

There's something, however, undeniably companionable about injuries. They seldom fail to occasion hilarity in one's teammates for two reasons: a) that could have been me, b) but it wasn't. One mishap that befell Rasputin last season certainly brought back warm memories of Frank Spencer.

It began when Rasputin broke a finger attempting a hot caught and bowled chance. He played on in discomfort, and postponed medical attention because that evening he was taking a girl he fancied on their first date. This went off swimmingly, but he woke next morning to find his hand looking like he'd forgotten to remove his batting glove. And when a doctor drilled into Rasputin's fingernail to relieve the pressure, both were showered in a geyser of blood.

At this point, things went really pear-shaped. Rasputin passed out, in the process banging his head so badly on a hospital trolley that he suffered months of headaches. Worse still, he couldn't remember the name of his date the previous evening. An anxious few days followed until Rasputin's phone rang at work.

'Were you intending to call me?' said a recognisable, rather querulous, female voice.

'I was,' replied Rasputin. 'Honestly. But first, can you tell me your name again?'

We laugh about this now because Rasputin's relationship subsequently prospered (if you're reading this Raz, her name is Maria). But, to be truthful, we got a fair bit of mileage out of it at the time as well—that's what injuries are for.

The commonest indispositions, naturally, are those that are self-inflicted. These intermittently occur at practice, when some wiseacre decides to rehearse their eighteen-yard bouncer or cranks the bowling machine up to 'Brett Lee'. More often they are hangovers, sometimes brought to the club, sometimes sponsored by it.

Our hippy paceman Castaway now takes precautions: he keeps a mattress at the club for the nights he can't quite stumble up the hill to snooze in his van. Even then, he can be difficult to rouse for a second spell. He was especially subdued after our recent karaoke night, probably from trying to interpret the lyrics to 'I Am the Walrus' at 5 a.m. through a brandy-induced haze.

To a degree, of course, all our mishaps are self-inflicted. They wouldn't occur and wouldn't matter, except that we play cricket. And the reasons aren't far to see. Most of us are crocks already. Our conception of a warm-up stretch is a yawn, a fag, and bending to tie our bootlaces; our idea of a youth policy is trying to do what we did at twenty. So here's another sense in which park cricket in Australia is a career. It's a career for doctors.

Week 15

Bats

A nice cameo at the weekend. A youthful opponent, probably sixteen or so, emerged for his innings with a bat that looked like it should have been in a cabinet behind glass at the MCG. CC sniffed a sledge in the making. 'That bat looks your granddad gave it to you,' he said.

'Actually,' the boy replied, 'he did.'

It was a beauty, too: light, sweetly sprung, dark with many loving applications of oil. On closer inspection it proved to be a Crockett, which makes it forty years old at least. How many boundaries had it belted in its lifespan? It struck another couple off me at the weekend. 'A privilege to be hit for four with such a bat,' I told the owner. Well, once in a while.

A cricketer with any soul *should* become a bit sentimental where bats are concerned. And, indeed, a lot of time at the Yarras is devoted to bats: thinking bats, talking bats, swapping bats and swinging bats—whether we know what to do with them or not. Womble's wand, for example, was handmade in New Zealand, is stencilled with his initials, weighs a ton, and makes not an iota of difference to the way he plays. He would be just as effective with a fencepost.

Big John has a fabled bat, 'Wonder Boy', repaired dozens of times and still swung in mighty arcs. And there does seem something slightly supernatural about it, given its owner's propensity for preparing for each innings with a joint.

Wonder Dog Two's 'The Original '95', meanwhile, may well be the most eye-catching of the lot. A short-handled paddle that he fashioned himself, it bears his name and a smart-looking cricket ball symbol of his own devising on the splice. We keep telling him that he's the most upwardly mobile number eleven in the business.

If all this seems fetishistic, fetishism about equipment is now almost mandatory, modern bats being composed of 10 per cent willow, 5 per cent rubber, and 85 per cent stickers. No longer does one seek out 'a Gray-Nicolls'; one now must distinguish between the Gray-Nicolls Millennium, Excalibur, Razor, Longbow and Stealth Bomber. Actually, I made the last one up, but you get the idea.

I'm not sure I like this. It made surveying the market a few years ago rather bemusing, at least at first. The Bubble Legend? Sounded like a spin-off series from 'Ab Fab'. The Ridgeback Intrigue? I thought that was a novel by Robert Ludlum. Mind you, it probably did make choosing a bit easier: by eliminating all bats with stupid names, I was left with a Slazenger V600. Which is excellent, if one is to judge by the quantities of runs that my colleagues have made with it.

Choosing the right bat is dependent on several factors: weight, pick-up, balance, aerodynamics. After all, if you're any sort of park cricketer, you'll throw it as much as swing it. My bat is now distinguishable from all other V600s by the deep indentation about half-way up the back, suffered on contact with a dressing-room bench at Dingley after a most egregious lbw dismissal. 'You should play that stroke more often,' said Chef, examining the damage at the club rooms later. 'At least it was an attacking shot.'

There's another vexing question about bats, which is what to do when they reach the end of their allotted span. Few of us at the Yarras have children—or, at least, children we know of—to whom our bats might be bequeathed. So what then? I've never been able to resolve this issue to my satisfaction. As a result, I've been followed in my travels for the last decade or so by an ever-expanding belfry of bats—old, battered and buggered.

A few Yarras guys sell their old bats to one another: what might be unfit for a self-respecting batsman may still be satisfactory for a self-disrespecting tail-ender. Otherwise it might be pooled in the club kit; a farrago of odd pads, worn-out gloves and broken stumps kept less for their general usefulness than as part of the pretence of being a cricket club.

A few years ago one of Malkovitch's old planks enjoyed a rather marvellous second life in the rambling shambles of the house shared with Bourkey, Easty and Gulbinator in Malvern. They took to it with a chisel from Bourkey's carpentry kit and ingeniously shaped it into a voluptuous female form, all hips and tits, which hung from the living-room wall.

This *objet de criquet*, a genuine fragment of vernacular folk art, used to fascinate me. It was more maternal than sensual, benign and abundant like an Etruscan fertility symbol. Alas, when I asked after it a few months ago, Malkovitch confessed that it had gone missing during the boys' eviction last year, one step ahead of the bulldozers—for which, it must be admitted, they had done some preparatory work.

The householders, he pointed out, *had* managed to salvage something from their former residence: two illuminated Victoria Bitter signs, knocked off from some pub in the dim, drunken past. Suitably tawdry, they now repose on the bar at Como Park. But Batgirl—who knows? I expect it will be discovered by some twenty-second-century anthropologist, who will classify it as a totem of an obscure religion. And they won't be completely wrong.

Week 16

Second Days

Saturday was the longest day of the year, and it felt like it. Having stumbled into a losing position a week ago by folding for 150, the First XI were absolutely thumped by Mordialloc, who made 350.

I was guesting. Pete Macca wanted a crafty slow bowler, and in the absence of same settled for me. And it was one of those days you dread all week which then unfolds precisely as projected. Rather like Christmas—so maybe it's good preparation.

This is the nature of the two-day cricket we play. It's great that everyone has the chance to succeed, not so great that everyone has the opportunity to fail—sometimes twice. The second day feels different to the first; you know approximately when you'll be batting and bowling; you know essentially whether you're in with a show, or negotiating the margin of defeat.

It's also in the nature of two-day cricket that you can bat in gloom one week and bowl in ethiopic heat the next, and that what was like an autobahn when you bowled the first Saturday has by the following Saturday become a length of the Birdsville Track.

Some years ago, in a game that at the Yarras will go down in infamy, we were fighting for a place in the finals against a club for whom the phrase 'trailer trash' would bring both trailers and trash into disrepute. Despite seven cloudless days between, what had been twenty-two yards of concrete for the first week was twenty-two yards of wet cement for the second. 'It was the council sprinklers wot dun it,' they explained cursorily; these being sprinklers of a particularly ingenious setting, capable of watering in a rectangular shape of sixty-six by five feet.

Everyone has a park cricket story like this—variations include blocks of ice on a length, patches of oil, and tyre tracks—but that made the occasion no more palatable. A game of pure spite ensued— *jihads* have been more polite—made worse by the jeers of a gang of cretinous kibbitzers. Our narrow defeat has since been memorialised in song by Dave Macca to the tune of 'American Pie'.

> A long, long time ago
> I can still remember when that cricket made me smile
> And I knew the Seconds had one more chance
> To join in on the finals dance
> And maybe win a premiership in fine style
> But February* made me shiver
> With the news that TB delivered
> Bad news at the wicket
> The——boys** decided to fix it
> I can't remember if I cried*** when a
> Good-length delivery hit my handle and skied
> And I headed off back inside
> The daaaay…that cricket…died
>
> And we were singing
> Bye bye——you know we hope you all die

* Yes, technically March.
** Oh yeah, the council. Sure.
*** I did.

> Drove for miles down the Nepean and found
> your pitch wasn't dry
> And your good ol' boys were drinking whisky
> and rye****
> Singing, 'This will be the day cricket died.'

The notes are Dave's, the sentiments universal.

Kicking off the second week is also slightly fraught for not-out batsmen. In my Yarras years there have been two instances of 'timed outs', both associated with restarts. Once this was sheer ineptitude. Nifty was a fair keeper, but a lawyer so notoriously disorganised that he must have driven judges crazy: 'I had hoped to address you, M'lud, on the grounds for clemency in my client's multiple homicide. I notice, however, that I have arrived with several volumes of case law concerning the illegal exportation of rare budgerigars. So you might as well give him the chair.'

Nifty seldom came equipped with more than one inner, and was always late, toting a cricket bag stuffed with briefs. This rarely mattered until one day at Royal Park when he forgot that he'd nightwatched the

---

**** Again, their cheer squad meatheads were technically drinking VB (what else?).

week before and arrived half an hour after start time.

Nifty didn't seem too perturbed: the idea of ensnarement by an obscure statute like Law 31, I suspect, rather appealed to his legal mind. 'Oh well,' he said, 'I'll have more time to read up on this case I've brought with me.' Delving into his bag, however, he began emitting grunts of frustration and annoyance. 'Fuck it!' he announced. 'I've brought the wrong one with me.'

The other instance, involving Laces, a handy bat, has entered the category of legend. At the end of the first Saturday, the Yarras were 1-25 chasing 150, with Laces already looking good on 15 not out on a pitch full of runs; so good, in fact, that he advised his parents to come and watch him bat the following weekend.

On the Friday night preceding the resumption, however, Laces totalled himself at a black-tie college ball. Hailing a cab, he was only capable of burbling 'Take me home'. The cabbie figured, not unreasonably, that the most suitable home was the Prahran lock-up.

Laces scarcely endeared himself to the constabulary by vomiting copiously all over himself and his cell. So when his mind began to clear, the police were disinclined to heed his pleas about an appointment to resume batting at Como Park at 1 p.m. So all was in readiness for a stirring knock by Laces that day—flat deck, hot day, and parents parked on a bench by the steps—save Laces himself. Time expired, and our skipper Staggy was obliged to recommence with a new batsman.

At the same time, the police were restoring Laces to liberty. And about twenty minutes later, a dishevelled figure in a vomit-streaked dinner jacket stumbled breathlessly down the steps from the top of the Como hill, passing his bug-eyed parents and running into his cold-eyed captain.

'Square leg!' Staggy barked. 'All day!' So Laces, formal attire increasingly whiffy, spent the day in umpiring purdah; Staggy even stood guard over the drinks tray so that the miscreant went unrefreshed. 'Nobody,' he said, 'but nobody, gives that bastard a drink!' I can't recall whether that was the longest day of the year; it was almost certainly the longest of Laces' life.

Week 17

Boxing Day

Trying to extract cash from an automated teller last week, I began to sense that the Yarras' season was taking its toll. What did it mean 'INCORRECT PIN'? Then it dawned, I'd been keying in Pete Macca's mobile telephone number. Perhaps, unconsciously, I was hoping that the machine would offer some selection advice.

Respite from Yarras responsibilities was, fortunately, round the corner: Christmas brings Melbourne park cricket to a fortnight's halt. Which is odd really. There's only one *bona fide* Christian at the Yarras: One Dad, a quick bowler prone to celebrating his wickets with a hearty 'Hallelujah!' He is, in any event, more than counterbalanced by Whirly, an orthodox Jew who scorns a helmet in favour of a yarmulke, and who bowls leg-breaks with an action resembling a man trying to sniff his own armpit.

On Melbourne's cricket calendar, though, Christmas really means little more than Boxing Day Test Match Eve, a prelude to the principal pilgrimage of the international summer. For the Yarras in town, attendance is not so much compulsory as compulsive. And for some of us, it requires a conscious act of restraint not to ford the boundary at lunch and join the pipsqueaks at their Kanga Cricket routines.

This Boxing Day, I had the company of nine-year-old Mitch, a friend's son making his Test spectating debut. Mitch's sporting soul was clearly up for grabs: he arrived wearing a New York Yankees shirt thrown over a Liverpool shirt which, after a trip to the official merchandise tent, was less tastefully but more patriotically covered by an Australia one-day uniform.

The next few hours would be crucial if cricket was to claim Mitch's allegiance. I even decided to induct him in the art of scoring, using spare pages at the back of the Yarras' 1999–2000 Seconds scorebook. 'This is something every good cricketer must learn to do, Mitch,' I said. 'No, don't look in the front of the book,

I had a bit of bad luck that season.'

'Steve Waugh doesn't have to keep the scores, does he?' Mitch inquired. 'And isn't he a good cricketer?'

Well, yes, I conceded. 'But if he didn't take his turn scoring, he wouldn't get a game at the Yarras. Not unless his wife made really good afternoon teas.' Then some sage advice: 'Better get some sunscreen on. Looks like it could be a bit warm today.'

Within minutes, the skies had opened, we were both wet through, and my phone began ringing like it was a selection night. Other Yarras teammates, scattered throughout the crowd, were checking my whereabouts and degree of exposure. Text messages from Moof and Womble, aloft in a sheltered eyrie of the Great Southern Stand, took particular pleasure in their chairman of selectors' sogginess.

Moof: U OK Chairman?

Me: Drenched.

Moof: Nice and dry up here. Shd have reserved seat ha ha.

Me: U R Dropped.

Moof: Womble offers open bowling.

Me: U R Undropped.

Deprived of cricket to score, Mitch kept tabs on my

phone traffic. We'd cracked double figures before play commenced, one call from my Hearters mate Evo on Queensland's Sunshine Coast, where it was 37 degrees, simply to inform me that he was on Queensland's Sunshine Coast, where it was 37 degrees—and that I wasn't.

'Why are all these people ringing you?' asked Mitch.

'Because they're my teammates, Mitch,' I explained. 'And they think it's funny that I'm wet and they're dry.'

'Why do they think it's funny?' Mitch continued, probing gently.

'Because they're my teammates, Mitch.' He looked puzzled. 'Because, errr, that's the sort of game cricket is.' He looked even more puzzled.

'What's a leg bye?' he then asked.

'Excellent question, Mitch,' I said.

Poor Mitch. I fear he ended the day convinced that Test cricket is a ceremony where 60,000 adults gather to sit hours in the rain bouncing mobile calls around. Nonetheless, he stuck gamely at his task during the brief intermissions of play, and only faltered for an over or two when his arm got tired. 'Scorers' elbow,

Mitch,' I consoled him. 'Happens to the best. Even at the Yarras.'

After a while, too, I relented, and relived a few matches from the 1999–2000 Yarras season documented in the front half of the scorebook. He happily accepted that all the sixes from my bowling had been mishits and all my dismissals lbw were gross miscarriages of justice. Kids, eh? You've gotta love 'em. Complete suckers.

One issue concerned me as stumps impended— would I be able to scrape enough money together to get us home? I remembered that our Firsts captain is on a hot punting streak. I'll ring Pete, I thought. He's pretty flush.

'Hallelujah!' as One Dad would say: as I was about to dial Pete's number, I suddenly remembered the code number for my plastic card. This break's been a tonic.

Outdoing the Don: A Scoreboard

Bill Andrews of Somerset entitled his memoirs *The Hand That Bowled Bradman* on the basis of only having dismissed the Don once, for 202, in 1938. So I feel no guilt about extracting a chapter from the day that I outscored the Don, even though it sort of, well, didn't actually happen.

I owe it all to Mitch, my Boxing Day companion, who put a damp baptism in Test cricket behind him the next day to stage a Test in his imagination and hone techniques recently trialled in the Yarras Seconds scorebook of 1999–2000. New Catland played Griff and Ar—a pun, apparently, on Mitch's dad's name (Griff) and Harry Potter's house (Gryffyndor)—and won a breathless contest.

As you will see on page 113, Haigh was run out 6. Must've been my call. But Bradman was still less successful, perhaps thanks to his recent cremation, and, as will be seen on page 115, succumbed first ball. His conqueror is not immediately obvious, it being either Chris Cairns, Andy Bichel, a CD-ROM character or a cat (see below).

Although I always take my turn scoring for the Yarras, I've never been much chop at it, since developing at school a species of maths anxiety—I have an abiding dread of two trains approaching each other, one at 60 kmh, one at 100 kmh. But there is something enchanting about a well-kept scoresheet. Gunbower, one of our Yarras opponents, has a book I always enjoy, as it's adorned with marginalia like 'untroubled gem' and 'what's this bloke doing at number three?'. Mitch, too, is a natural. A lovely hand. Attention to detail, but no fear of subjective judgment: notice the allusive analysis in Superman's first over. Plus, he knows how to take care of his mates, which means he will probably make a good chairman of selectors too.

Some pen pics are required, and I'm grateful to Mitch's mum Philippa for her explications of those contestants who were beyond my ken.

NEW CATLAND

1. P. Sanchaz

Pablo. Outstanding player in a Humungous CD-ROM game, Backyard Baseball. May have had some trouble adapting to a different set of rules and set off for a run to where he thought first base was.

2. M. Clemens

Mitch. What sort of imaginary cricket game is it in which you don't top score?

3. Cairns

Chris of that ilk. Mitch's favourite cricketer. Good choice.

4. Leeu

Small furry lemur toy which Mitch had been given for Christmas.

5, 6, 7. Pollock, Ntini, Haigh

'No explanation needed,' Philippa remarks, 'for these three giants of the game.'

8. Crookshanks

Cat owned by Mitch's sister Greer, named for the ginger in *Harry Potter*.

9. Bichel

Blond cricketer.

NEW CATLAND CRICKET CLUB v. GRIF AND R C. CLUB

HOME CLUB: NEW CATLAND
2nd Ist INNINGS OF NEW CATLAND .... PLAYED AT THE SULLIVAN PARK **ON** 24/7/12/ **200**1.

BATSMAN	TIME IN / OUT	1 2 3 4 5 6 7 8 9 10	HOW OUT	BOWLER	TOTAL
1 PANCHAZ		1 3 >>	RUN OUT	SUPERMAN	1
2 M. CLEMENS		4 2 >>	CAUGHT	SUPERMAN	7
3 CAIRNS		3 4	BOWLED	SNAPE	6
4 LEEU		2	CAUGHT	SNAPE	3
5 POLLOCK		*	RUN OUT		4
6 NTINI			BOWLED	SUPERMAN	1
7 HAIGH			RUN OUT		0
8 CROOKSHANKS		GOLDEN DUCK	LBW	SUPER	6
9 BUCHER			NOT OUT		0
10 SHEVCHENKO		3	RUN OUT		
11 POO-CHI			BOWLED	SPY FOX	

RUNS AT THE FALL OF EACH WICKET AND NO. OF OUTGOING BATSMAN
1 2 3 4 5 6 7 8 9 10

BYES
LEG BYES
WIDES
NO BALLS

BOWLING ANALYSIS
11 12 13 14 15 16 17 18 19 20 21 22 23 24

EXTRAS
TOTAL
FOR WICKETS

BOWLERS	1 2 3 4 5 6 7 8 9 10 ...
1 SUPERMAN	2 ? *
2 SNAPE	: :
3 SPY FOX	
4	
5	
6	
7	
8	

UMPIRES 1 POO-CHI 2 MARTY   **SCORERS** 1   2

GAME STARTED
GAME FINISHED
RESULT

10. Shevchenko
Andriy, AC Milan's charismatic no. 7. Mitch's favourite footballer.
11. Poo-Chi
Nasty plastic robo dog. Appears to have umpired while his team batted. Paul Condon to investigate.

GRIFF AND AR

1. Boon
Taswegian divinity.
2. Duck
Daffy, not Donald, apparently.
3. Bradman
Name of museum. Pah!
4. Warne
Blond cricketer.
5. G. Clemens
Griff. Mitch's dad.
6. Snape
Severus. Enigmatic potions master in *Harry Potter*, who dislikes chief protagonist and clearly got what he deserves.
7. Phar Lap
People's champion.

NEW CATLAND CRICKET CLUB v. GRIFF AND AR........ C. CLUB

HOME CLUB FIRST INNINGS OF GRIFF AND AR. PLAYED AT THE KITCHEN ON 27/12/01

	BATSMAN	TIME IN/OUT												HOW OUT	BOWLER	TOTAL
1	BOON		>>GOLDEN DUCK													0
2	DUCK		>>GOLDEN DUCK													0
3	BRADMAN		>>golden DUCK													0
4	WARNE		4													4
5	G. Chappell		21													3
6	SNAPE		61.4.5>>GOLDEN DUCK													0
7	PH.ARLAP													RUN OUT		2
8	SPY FOX		>>GOLDEN DUCK													0
9	ARNOLD		7											NOT OUT		7
10	SUBERMAN		>>GOLDEN DUCK													0
11	P.J. SAM		>>GOLDEN DUCK													0

BYES
LEG BYES
WIDES
NO BALLS 1

EXTRAS 1
TOTAL 25
FOWs WICKETS

BOWLING ANALYSIS

BOWLERS																									OVERS	MDNS	RUNS	WKTS
1	CAIRNS																								6	1	1	3
2	CROOKSHANK																								6	0	2	4
3	SAGHAZ																								6	0	7	1
4	BICHEL																								10	1	0	2

UMPIRES   GATES   CLEM RN'S   2   SCORERS 1

8. Spy Fox
International Fox of Mystery from Humungous CD-ROM game.

9. Arnold
Eponymous football-headed protagonist of the 'Hey Arnold!' cartoon series.

10. Superman
Evergreen action hero.

11. PJ Sam
Another alumnus of Humungous CD-ROM game.

It will come as no surprise that Mitch is a bowler. There is a flourish, a *Schadenfreude*, about those emphatic 'Golden Ducks'. I think he has a bright future ahead of him, and there is another reason that he will be a natural for the Yarras: like ours, his scores don't add up.

Week 18

Home

Is there such a thing as home-ground advantage? Watch the Brisbane Lions at the Gabba and you think there must be. Cast your mind back to the Brisbane Bears at Carrara, however, and there seems a solid case for home ground disadvantage as well.

So the fact that the Yarras Fourth XI are unbeaten at Como Park this season—after another solid home win at the weekend against the formidable Powerhouse—may be meaningless. After all, F-Troop had an unbeaten record within the precincts of Fort Courage. But I suspect a few other factors have played a part.

Pitches at Como have seldom been of the best. Our batsmen used to complain that they were the only minefield victims in the world not to be consoled by a visit from Princess Di, while the practice decks crumbled so routinely that they were referred to as 'Bombay', 'Port-of-Spain' and 'Sydney'. ('Can you bat in Sydney tonight, Moof?' 'Yeah, OK. It's a bit hot in Bombay anyway.')

Last year, in fact, we became fed up enough to go looking for a new pitch doctor. And Bomber—a barrel-chested bricklayer in winter, and a green-thumbed groundsman in summer—has been a godsend.

Bomber was a tough-as-nails fast bowler in his playing days for Middle Park, and has kept the attitude, if not the speed. He seems, to a greater or lesser degree, to hate every other team in the competition. 'They're a pack of pricks,' he'll say. 'But they're not quite as bad as that other pack of pricks. They're a *real* pack of pricks.'

The pitches Bomber has prepared at Middle Park, though, have always been of a quality that Tony Greig would be privileged to stick his car keys in. A deal for him to take care of Como Park was cut in five minutes, and Yarras skippers now spend longer thinking about whether to call 'heads' or 'tails' than what to do if the option they choose comes up.

Oddly enough, opposition captains don't seem to have twigged. A feature of Bomber's pitches is that they often look grassy; this is because our clapped-out mower—rather like a few of our fielders—finds it hard getting down as low as it used to. Visitors sometimes think 'greentop', and send us in; we know 'rock bottom' and suppress a smile. Bomber, of course, is affronted that any captain would do other than bat on winning the toss ('They did that? What a pack of pricks!').

The Como outfield, meanwhile, is a tricky one. It has a slight downward grade from the Dogshit End to the Sahara End, and also changes character markedly as the season progresses—2 in October will streak for 4 in January, as the grass dries, the pitches flatten and the front-foot bullies prosper.

The outfield, though, is at its slowest in December. This is because the council—which treats us rather like a caravan of importunate gypsies—want the ground aesthetically lush for Carols by Candlelight. We're not unsympathetic—after all, we love karaoke—but it does affect calculations. Scoring in December has to be adjusted according to the 'Carols Index': 200 'cum Carols', for example, is worth 250 'ex Carols'.

Another Como characteristic is that it's a mini-maidan. While the pavilion side is a clearly marked perimeter, the far side overlaps with another field used by Prahran Thirds and Fourths in VCA Premier Cricket. That the arena's intersecting portion is occupied by fielders facing in opposite directions, involved in different matches, is actually quite congenial; when proceedings on your ground are dull, you can sort of channel-surf between games by turning around. But a result of this is that sloggers swipe with greater alacrity towards the pavilion side, the visible boundary, than towards the less-distinct far side, seemingly patrolled by about fifteen men. This is local knowledge that no spinner can do without.

The greatest home-ground advantage that we enjoy at Como Park, however, is its scenic beauty. The hill, the river and the trees can't help but inculcate a glad-to-be-alive feeling, and have been an important drawcard for players. Our veteran's veteran Hicksy explains that his career at the club began simply because he drove past one day and thought, 'Hey, I wouldn't mind playing cricket there.' Twenty-four seasons later, he still is.

It's pleasant, too, to show off the ground. Over the

years, I've brought many friends and acquaintances down to Como, and the response is always the same. 'Gee, lovely ground,' they say. 'You must play a high standard of cricket here.' I don't encourage them to watch too closely.

Week 19

Fantasy

When you're a club cricketer, you often wonder how good you are. Should you give up, pack it in and recycle your old abdominal protector as a cufflinks holder? Or are you just 'a good player out of luck'?—albeit in my case for about twenty-five years. At last, such musings are over. How good am I?— $17,900.

This is the value imputed to me in the latest Yarras wheeze: a Fantasy League. Practised football fantasists know the routine. You purchase a virtual team, members valued on the basis of past performances, with a pretend purse, up to an agreed limit. Then you wait for them to be either injured, sacked, appear in a Guy Ritchie film or marry a Spice Girl.

In our competition, there is the additional complication of actually playing alongside our selections. Wogger is unlikely now to wed a Spice Girl—you don't meet many pop divas while wiping the vomit off drunks at the casino. But he is endangered by my running between wickets: to my chagrin, endangered by three yards at the weekend, shortly after I'd spent $24,000 virtual cash acquiring him for my choice XI.

Nonetheless, the response to the Yarras Fantasy League has already been overwhelming. It's a very clever system that uses the same software as the ResultsVault package devised for us by Pete and Dave Macca. And, as Dave says, 'I told Pete it was a fucked idea that would never work and just ignored him. So I guess you'd call it a joint invention.' Forty-two players have entered teams in what is being promoted as 'your chance to be chairman of selectors'—demonstrating an alacrity entirely absent whenever the real chairmanship of selectors has been up for grabs.

Naturally, the task bears little resemblance to my fortnightly ordeal with player list, needle and blindfold. Entrants in the Yarras Fantasy League, for instance, are required to pick a perfectly balanced XII: six batsmen, a keeper, two all-rounders, three bowlers.

This might be an ideal configuration in theory, but vicissitudes of availability always militate against it in practice. When Melbourne's spring racing carnival was inducing an epidemic of twinged hamstrings and strained groins late last year, for example, my co-selectors and I had to sign off on a Fourth XI containing two batsmen, four keepers, three bowlers, and two nuff-nuffs. But I guess that's why it's called a Fantasy League, and it certainly has the boys talking.

The formula on which Pete Macca relies to calculate individual values is already the subject of some conjecture. It appears to be based on the PriceWaterhouseCoopers Rankings, crossed with the Duckworth-Lewis System and integrated with Fermat's Last Theorem—then multiplied by zero and replaced by a figure arbitrarily plucked from the air so as to place Pete somewhere near the top.

'I can't understand why I'm only worth $7500,' complained Womble last week. 'There must be something wrong with Pete's maths.'

'Don't ask me,' I replied. 'I'm still coming to terms with being called an "all-rounder". I think it means "does nothing particularly well".' If Womble was seriously concerned, I suggested he consider relocating to

Argentina, where his value would be guaranteed to inflate ten-fold in a week.

You can now see players at practice sniffing for bargains, mentally noting those who seem to be hitting a spot, and in for a long time rather than a good time. McFly has just returned from a holiday in South America and is spanking them everywhere in the nets. Sixteen thousand dollars? Sold! Wilson's only made two runs in three innings this season after a long absence from the game, but I've glimpsed a vestigial cover drive taking shape in the nets. Two thousand dollars? A snip! Fearless punters have been taking a chance on Apu, three digs for four runs before he was delegated night shifts at his service station, but he's still worth a flutter at $1000 if his arms aren't too tired from serving Slurpies when he returns. There's also jostling at the blue chip end of the market between our three top-priced fast bowlers, Wonder Dog Two ($40,000), Humphrey ($38,300) and Moof ($38,000). This is good news for the rest of us, as they are now too busy bouncing each other to bother anybody else.

Players are also spending hours over their permutations and combinations, for obtaining the maximum bang for your buck is quite a teasing arithmetic exercise. Humphrey has actually spent every permissible penny of the allocated $190,000—this is understandable, as he works in finance. It may likewise be revealing that the three cheapest outfits are those assembled by Fat Tony, Mulva and myself—respectively the Yarras' treasurer, secretary and vice-president. In a Yarras context, you become frugal even with virtual money.

Finding an apt designation for your chosen XI is perhaps most demanding of all. In my case, the Hesketh Naylers honours the sesquicentenary of a New York millionaire who, according to J. L. Carr's *Dictionary of Extraordinary Cricketers*, derived sexual gratification from watching fat naked women bat and bowl with balloons—remember, we are talking cricket fantasies here. The uniting principle of Rasputin's Rasta Nuns of the Revelations, Wilson's One-Ton Sucker Muckers and Malkovitch's Chicks with Dicks is even more elusive—so perhaps it's safer that they've passed me over.

At least as intriguing as one's nominal dollar value is learning where you stand in teammates' thoughts. It's flattering, albeit in a back-handed way, to have been chosen by Knackerbags, the Pie Chuckers and Could've Been Champions, while I regard inclusion in Wogger's Warriors as testimony to his forgiving nature. And I should be thankful not to have been drafted by any of Me and Me Bitches, Hakattack, the Custard Arms, the Moe Kidnappers, Thommo's Tufnells, and Marty's Middle-Order Collapses.

On the contrary, I'll think of it as a spur. Time to prove the doubters wrong. Viva le Hesketh Naylers! In any case, I don't own any cufflinks.

Week 20

Duffers

As darkness closed in on a balmy Saturday with the Yarras still toasting their afternoon's successes last week, a kookaburra descended on the balcony at our Como Park home and loosed its joyous cry. Taking aim, Moof narrowly missed it with his boot. 'No one laughs at us and gets away with it,' he explained.

It being January, club affairs have become somewhat serious. Not hugely so, and certainly not Steve-Waugh-sleep-with-your-baggy-green-and-write-a-turgid-tour-diary-about-it serious. But, as we fantasise of finals and flags come March, training has grown more robust and eyes a little beadier, while selection meetings have become rather more like poker, and a little less like 52-Pickup.

We had a classic dilemma recently, involving X, a complete fuck-all-rounder for whom square leg is more physical description than fielding position, and Y, an outstanding batsman who retired last season but who'd unexpectedly inquired about a game (it's unfair to name either, in case this is read by X, who does try exceedingly hard, or by Y's wife, who still believes he was visiting a sick uncle).

Both Doc and Churchyard, respectively Thirds and Fourths captains, wanted Y, but wouldn't countenance X. 'He's got all the cricket sense of a stump,' opined Doc of X. 'You only have to watch him in the field. He stands there like he's holding on for a crap.'

Churchyard was equally emphatic. 'I refuse to captain a player who even drops the ball when it's handed to him.'

This bickering continued on and off for some hours. Players usually linger for the reading of the teams on Thursday night, but sensing the deliberations' gravity this particular evening they didn't hang around.

At about 10.30 p.m., Pete Macca interposed. 'Right, that's it. I'm linking X and Y,' he said. 'Whoever takes Y gets X. It's a buy-one-get-one-free deal. If you want

Buns of Steel, you have to take the free set of steak knives whether you want 'em or not. Just stick 'em in the bottom drawer and, if anyone comments, pretend they were there when you moved in.'

Churchyard finally buckled. 'Bugger it, I'll put X at slip. We haven't held anything there this season anyway,' he rationalised. In the end, X did quite well, even removing his hands from his pockets occasionally.

It's not, of course, that the Yarras are any academy of excellence. After all, this is the club where a fast bowler once requested he be relieved because he'd just realised his pants were on back-to-front, and where a slow bowler sprained an ankle tripping over a net cord (um, that was me). It's just that there are a few Yarras cricketers classified 'only to be used in case of emergency' for whom opportunities will henceforward be limited.

There's Swanny, whose leggies would only be effective on an eleven-yard pitch. There's Wock, whose Yarras batting career spans one delivery, from which he was bowled and hit wicket. There's Penfold, whom I've never seen play, but whose proudest boast is that he once acted as twelfth man to a Yarras team containing ten men. Then there's Space Cadet, whom I wouldn't mind picking, but who suffers from a reputation for eccentricity: hence the nickname.

Spacer is actually a very interesting guy, in a New Age kind of way, and brings to the club a vast store of knowledge on hypnosis and Russian breathing techniques. Watto, who joined us from the spartan regime of the district club Prahran, recalls that Spacer was the first Yarras cricketer he introduced himself to at practice.

'What do you do?' Watto asked ingenuously.

'I teach Tibetan throat singing,' Spacer answered.

Watto then spied Castaway, looking like the lost Doobie brother, thundering up to bowl in a pair of Blundstones, and thought he had walked into the Age of Aquarius.

Spacer's cricket is a concatenation of quirks. With a range of late cuts and reverse sweeps, he seems to place the ball according to the signs of the zodiac, and bowls right-arm all sorts of staggering variety. Six balls of an over from Spacer will be different in every respect: run-up, action, follow-through, result.

Sadly, the skippers seem to hold aesthetic reservations about Spacer. They admit he can be heretically effective, it's just that, if he's playing the right way, everyone else is wrong. When I e-mailed Pete Macca a draft XI including Space Cadet recently, he returned it with the notation, 'Further moonwalk practice necessary'.

This will puzzle some readers. After all, Australia is meant to be the country where cricket is bred in the bone and there is 'no such thing as a social game'. In my experience, though, this has always been Aussie *amour propre*. Every club I've represented has contained a proportion of make-up-the-numbers cases, whose prime condensed to the few seconds in which they took a catch a decade ago, and whose contribution to the team effort is an eleventh pair of trousers for ball-polishing. Indeed, they've often been popular club men, creating a small buffer zone between one's self and abject hopelessness.

It's simply that, in January, you begin reflecting it mightn't be an altogether retrograde step if catches off your bowling went at least to hand rather than elbow, knee or chest. And that if there's laughing to be done it should be yours, not the opponents', and not the local fauna's.

Week 21

Joy

All of us at the Yarras endure phases of disillusionment, where the idea of preserving our small, intermittently successful, permanently broke club seems hardly worth the candle—by comparison, in fact, the candle looks worth betting your life savings on.

Forgive us, then, our periods of illusionment, when if cut we'd bleed Yarra blue. Last weekend was one such. There hasn't been so much laughter at Como Park since the committee last looked at the club finances.

On Saturday, the Fourths were involved in a sublime game of cricket, winning a one-day fixture outright in enervating heat, with everything going uncannily, almost eerily, right. Boundaries flowed in unending profusion. Sharp catches lodged in hands that might arrest a ball once a season. Captain Churchyard, a very unwilling keeper whose gloves normally come together like a pair of cymbals, even chested a stumping.

As the Fantasy League fortunes of Wogger's Warriors and the Hesketh Naylers prospered from our own and each others' performances, Wogger and I suffered sore hands from high-fiving so often. You'd put up with a season in which you were hit for nothing but sixes and suffered a string of dodgy lbws just to play in such a match—and I should know because I nearly have.

Towards the end, the atmosphere was literally electric, with lightning forking the sky as Canterbury's tail strove to stave us off. And no sooner had we inflicted the *coup de grâce* than the heavens opened. Beneath the arboreal shelter of Fawkner Park we watched the rain sheet down. It was as sweet as our victory, the sort of moment you wanted to last forever. That evening, as the Fourths celebrated their unaccustomed altitude at the top of the ladder, the lights burned late at Como Park—though not quite as late as the following evening.

On Sunday, we hosted a charity match to raise funds for the enviromental trust fund constituted in memory of our 2000–1 Fourth XI captain, AB. The environmental aspect of the event, I suspect, had limited impact—park cricketers tend to think of the greenhouse effect as an entirely sensible objective. But the idea of honouring AB was as popular as the man himself, and a hundred or so witnessed the South Yarra All-Stars, led by AB's father Ron and brothers Mick and Richard, taking on the Clean, Green EPA Machine, led by Castaway and composed of AB's former colleagues at the Environment Protection Authority.

The right tone was struck at once when Womble was adjudged lbw for the misdemeanour of consecutive defensive shots. The appeal echoed round Como Park, uniquely in my experience, from both opponents and teammates, and AB's former boss Terry gave a vox populi decision. Indeed, Terry adjudicated with superb subjectivity all day, at one point lecturing us: 'Any player who doesn't like the standard of umpiring here can go and find another game…another game where the umpire doesn't cheat so much.'

Womble later got his own back by bowling

Castaway, his first wicket at the club for ten years. Not to be upstaged, Moof cover-drove a six while batting left-handed, touching off an epidemic of leftupmanship without which no social match is complete. It fell to me to ensure that another unwritten convention of social matches was also fulfilled—the etiquette that at least one man must be bowled by a girl (otherwise known as the Lara Law). The charming Selena from EPA found a challenging length half-way down the pitch and I was beaten by the roll. It's a novel experience to be able to turn and watch the ball bump the stumps with just enough residual ergs to dislodge a bail. 'I assume that was deliberate,' proposed Panther.

'At some level,' I philosophised, 'all dismissals are deliberate.'

After a lunchbreak that sprawled an hour and a half, the Yarras coasted to a comfortable victory, and Ron Burnell accepted our newly minted AB Memorial Match shield with a brief but moving speech. How deeply we've missed him; how good it was that we could remember him so. My cobber Evo from Sacred Heart—the Yarras' favourite rivals—also announced that the Mercantile Cricket Association C-Grade Best and Fairest award for the season was to be renamed in our old mate's honour. I wonder if Eddie McGuire would be interested in hosting *our* AB Medal?

A long day then turned into a longer evening on the Como Park pavilion balcony, until the fridge was picked clean and the barbecue was depleted to its last cubic centimetre of gas. Wogger, Bourkey, Malkovitch and Castaway declined to depart at all and kipped in the club rooms. And if you'll forgive such maudlin sentimentality, the feeling around the Yarras on the day can't be explained entirely by collective incoherence. It's remarkable how promising the future can seem when it's hard enough recalling the immediate past. It's amazing how right the world can look when it's not quite in focus.

This could be a proper turning point in our season, as distinct from our usual simultaneous turning points which result in us ending up where we started. But we'll be keeping the candle to hand, just in case we can't come up with the cash to cover the next electricity bill.

Umpires: An Inquiry

An established cricket principle holds that it's virtually impossible to adjudge a batsman lbw when a left-arm inswing bowler is operating from round the wicket, especially when that batsman is taking a leg stump guard, and when his pad flap is merely grazed by the ball's passage through to the keeper. But it just so happens... Well, you know what I'm about to say, don't you?

Like Clive of India, I stood amazed by my own moderation. 'Upon my soul, Mr Umpire,' I observed to the official, 'I have certainly never been given out like that before.'

'I can assure you, Mr Batsman,' replied the umpire, 'that the delivery concerned straightened.'

'If the delivery concerned straightened to the degree that you imply, Mr Umpire,' I remarked, 'then the bowler concerned should be playing for Australia.' Actually, this is just the gist of our conversation. I was kidding about the moderation.

The man in white is, of course, always right—irrespective of his being, at the Yarras' level of the game, often ancient, astigmatic, deaf and disorganised. It's just that one must sometimes be patient, on the occasions when the man in white's rightness is not immediately obvious.

Everything a cricketer says of umpires should be taken with a grain of salt. A common park cricketers' lament is, 'I don't really care about how good the umpire is, as long as he's consistent'. By which is meant, in this context, 'consistent in giving *us* not out and giving *them* out'. In park cricket, nonetheless, it takes a certain type of person to want to stand there and be shouted at all day for $80 or so. And we do get those certain types.

The ump we've seen most of this season, for instance, clearly enjoys his avocation. Pat Pending rejects lbw appeals with a dismissive 'get-outta-here' drawl ('NOT AHHHTT!!'), while his calling of no balls is a mini-oratorio ('BAAAALLLL!!'). This has Torqs, our short-fused and ever-so-slightly-paranoid paceman, completely spooked. The sight of Pat fills him with dismay—'Oh no, not this bastard again'—and he'll run willingly into the teeth of a gale in order to bowl at the other end.

Then there's Legless Les. The epithet makes one aspect of his habits fairly clear, but his relish of umpiring is equally obvious. Just as players enjoy recounting the day's events over a beer or two, Legless revels in reliving his decisions over a slab or two. One evening at Como, I watched Legless explain to our president TB at least six times why he'd been given out lbw that day. No player describing an unplayable outswinger or sweetly struck six could have done so in such rhapsodic terms.

Legless was the last man to leave that night, by which time nobody was unenlightened about TB's method of dismissal some hours earlier. 'It's getting late, Les,' I explained slowly. 'I'm going to have to close the bar now.' A look of pleading crossed his face: 'But I haven't told you about the caught behind…'

Undoubtedly the oddest umpire the Yarras have encountered, however, was Ratso. A short, stocky, slightly seedy character, he had a few problems with his concentration, not to mention his personal hygiene. He tended to nod off at square leg, and was wont to expedite the tea-break because of nicotine withdrawal.

For a few years, we seemed to get Ratso every match, and he was known to like a chat—the more so with me when he found out I wrote for a living. Ratso, it emerged, nourished writing ambitions himself, which he enjoyed sharing, in somewhat surreal fashion. On one occasion, I was standing at square leg when he asked, 'Doing any writing?'

'Oh, a bit,' I said.

'I've been writing, too,' he said proudly.

'Really? What have you been concentrating on?'

'I've been writing songs.'

'I didn't know you could write music, Ratso.'

'I can't.'

I was already in way too deep, but I had to press on. 'So,' I conjectured, 'does that mean you've been writing poetry?'

'No, songs.'

'I see. But without music.'

'No.'

'Right,' I said. 'Why are you writing these songs?'

'I want to do a musical.' Ratso sounded very proud.

There you have it: the world's first musical without music. But then, Ratso may also be the first person to enforce the game's laws without consulting them. A season or two later, I bowled a ball that pitched perhaps a whisker outside off stump, turned maybe a couple of whiskers, and struck the batsman's back ankle directly in front.

It was almost adding to the batsman's embarrassment to appeal, but I did anyway. Gobsmackingly, Ratso failed to respond. 'Err, Ratso,' I suggested, 'just to remind you: for "out", you stick your right index finger in the air.'

'The batsman is not out,' Ratso proclaimed. 'The ball pitched outside off stump.'

'Hey ump!' interposed Wally from cover. 'It doesn't have to pitch in line if it hits in line.'

'I'm telling you that it's not out,' insisted Ratso. 'Let's get on with the game.'

I cursed myself for not having been more enthusiastic about his music-free songs. Then, standing at square leg a few overs later, I overheard him chuckling to himself. 'Y'know, one of these days I've really gotta look up that lbw law.'

Lbw is the law that sorts all umpires out, and it is imposed in our competition in a pretty speculative fashion. A time-honoured Yarras gesture involves one hand forming the outline of a gun, the other spinning an imaginary chamber, meaning it's Russian Roulette time—which you suffer as a batsman and try exploiting as a bowler. But it's hard to complain too much about umpiring. It's an inexact science. And in that sense, it fits well with our supremely inexact cricket.

Week 22

Sledging

The Yarras isn't a club where suits are often seen, except maybe crumpled at the bottom of someone's cricket bag. So the sight of Churchyard, Torqs and myself looking like a trio of Mormon doorknockers in Fawkner Park last Wednesday night was most incongruous.

As a matter of fact, it was a momentary lapse into seriousness for us. We were headed for the Mercantile Cricket Association's tribunal, where Torqs was to answer a charge of 'persistent sledging'—which, given this country's reputation, may strike some readers as analagons to an allegation of 'persistent breathing'.

Actually sledging is quite difficult to write about in Australia—not so much because it's a controversial subject, but because it's a cliche. It's tiresome to hear Aussie players drone on about it being 'part and parcel of cricket', like somebody arguing that road rage is 'part and parcel of driving'. Nor do I derive much satisfaction from the musing that cricket owes England the googly, India the leg-glance, Pakistan reverse swing, and Australia the phrase 'you're fucking shit'. But frankly, if you want to play cricket here, you accept sledging, just as if you want to use e-mail, you deal with spam.

Now and again, you still hear a funny sledge. A few games ago in the Fourths, Wogger was having trouble with an opening batsman who couldn't lay a stick on him. Studying the opponent's bat, a cleanskin bare of stickers, he groaned, 'No wonder you haven't got a sponsor.' Likewise, when the Seconds encountered a left-arm spinner before Christmas who insisted on bowling in a tight-fitting terry-towelling hat, TB felt moved to ask: 'What's the condom on your head for? Are you practising safe bowling?' Good to see the president setting an example.

Yet most sledging in park cricket is, well, bovine in its stupidity—of the 'You're shit'—'Am not'—'Are too'—'Am not'—'Are too' variety. Players know it as well, and try to compensate for its stupidity through sheer repetitiveness. It's gotten to the extent, in fact, where sledging might have had its day; it's now a bore rather than a real competitive edge. Perhaps it would make a difference if I was a better player. But being told I can neither bat nor bowl—or, more accurately, neither fucking bat nor fucking bowl—doesn't seem a terribly challenging remark.

Thus, in an iniquitous world, I find the issue of sledging difficult to get into a lather about. I personally don't sledge; this in all honesty is probably less an ethical decision than an admission that I've a hard enough time concentrating on what I'm meant to be doing without also thinking of something to say.

The fact that Torqs *is* inclined to dish it out has also never seriously disturbed me either. He's a fast bowler, and they've all got a screw loose somewhere. Indeed, the gratuitous advice in which he'd indulged during the relevant game was barely out of the ordinary for Torqs, whose head gets so hot when he bowls that you could fry an egg on it—which would go pretty well with the chips on his shoulders. You can talk to Torqs all you like, but it's all down to him. As the baseballer Paul Owens put it: 'You can lead a horse to water, but you can't stick his head in it.'

The Mercantile Cricket Association, though, is a pretty friendly competition, and its hardworking secretary, Simon Phillips from Gunbower, tries to keep it that way. Fawkner Park, as he points out, is a favoured location for weekend constitutionals, which aren't much enriched by a chorus of distant effing and blinding. Hence Churchyard's presence, as captain from the match, and mine, as vice-president, to project an image of rectitude and responsiveness on the club's part. Pity about the suit being covered in cat fur when I retrieved it from the floordrobe, but it was dark anyway.

The week leading up to the hearing had been a little tense. First, Torqs wasn't going to show up; he was through with cricket anyway and might as well go out with a defiant bang. Then, he was planning a defence case to rival O. J. Simpson's—the umpires and Simon Phillips had it in for him and he'd never get a fair hearing. Fortunately, Alan Dershowitz wasn't available. And frankly, these things *do* happen. Pebbles, the devoted statistician and factotum at our rivals Burnley, told me that as club secretary he once had to take an entire team to the tribunal, all of them having been reported for dissent. I'm surprised this has not made *Wisden*.

As it turned out, the tribunal hearing this night was perfectly fair. And having gone in like a lion, Torqs testified like a lamb. He even stomached pleading guilty, which was a manful concession from him, and gave a convincing impression of contrition. Churchyard and I then said a few words in his favour before the imposition of a two-week sentence suspended until the end of the next season.

'Reckon you can keep your innermost thoughts to yourself for a while Torqs?' I asked as we three suits stumbled off into the night. 'Yeah yeah,' he said. 'I'll be OK. It'll be good for me.'

'I hope you can do it,' said Churchyard. 'Because you know who we're playing this weekend? Gunbower. Simon Phillips' boys.'

Maybe I should take my suit to the dry cleaners.

Week 23

Dog

Success has a thousand fathers, which is probably why nobody at the Yarras can quite recall how, a year ago, we acquired our club greyhound, Six Bits. It simply happened, probably after a boozy Saturday night when a remark about the club 'going to the dogs' would have been ripe for misinterpretation.

Anyway, we've got him, though for how much longer is unclear. Last Saturday was, as Pete Macca put it, 'do or die for Six Bits'. Suffice it to say he didn't.

The initiative began, like so many at the Yarras, amid unquenchable enthusiasm. Before we knew it, a dozen of us were $150 lighter, and Pete and our leg-spinner Chef had identified an acquisition in rural Traralgon. They might have had second thoughts when the vendor proved not to be a prosperous figure in a plaid jacket and pork-pie hat but someone called Nobby who stacked supermarket shelves. And they should have had third thoughts when the dog urinated and vomited all over the car on the journey home.

But we were chuffed. The Yarras have long dreamed of a cash cow; a cash dog might do as well. We named the animal after a popular park cricket cry for the hit over the boundary on the full: 'That's six bits!' He was paraded round Como Park, and packed off to a rearer then a breaker to encourage an aptitude for what we regard as second nature: going endlessly in circles.

Alan the breaker was, alas, not supportive—there aren't many shades of ambiguity about 'disgraceful'. Thus the moment of truth, a barrier trial a few hours before we were scheduled to play our games, which Chef, Pete, DK and I decided to attend. 'Maybe we should take a present,' suggested Chef as we commenced the fifty-kilometre drive to Six Bits' lodgings in Lara. 'Have we got any rabbits?' Pete glanced at DK, who collected a 'pair' in his last game: 'DK's here.'

En route, Chef explained how coursing had first

captivated him. One beery betting afternoon in his local, he backed a dog that the race announcer mysteriously failed to mention in his call. Chef's hope, it was revealed, was still slavering in his stall, having been shoved in the wrong way. 'It's a sign,' Chef thought. 'I've gotta own me one o' them things.'

At last, we arrived at the Lara Greyhound Education Centre, a prepossessing address for an unprepossessing location: a track ringed by corrugated iron and a row of kennels, one of them occupied by Six Bits. It was a touching reunion, Six Bits in his excitement apparently overcome by delirium tremens. 'Save it, boy,' Macca said soothingly. 'Save it for the track.'

'Give him one of your famous First XI pep talks,' I suggested.

'OK guys,' Macca mumbled. 'We've lost six in a row. Gotta win this one. But I know you're a bunch of soft cocks, so let's go out and get this over with.'

Alan then arrived to field our questions, explaining that Six Bits had just finished 'spelling'.

'This *is* a thorough "education centre",' I mused. 'When does he start maths?'

'Spelling means resting,' Alan said.

'I knew that,' I replied.

We watched hopefully as Six Bits was shoved into a starting stall, more hopefully as he bolted after the lure…then ruefully as he lost interest after a hundred yards, doubled back, wandered into Alan's yard, and deposited a large pile of business. 'He does that a lot,' commented Alan.

'So do some of our players,' replied Chef.

Next we witnessed what a greyhound is supposed to do. A lean black streak exploded from the start, screamed round the circuit, then ravenously gored the lure—a real rabbit; very ragged, very dead. 'Do you think Six Bits was watching?' I asked Pete.

'Nah,' he said. 'Head in a book, as always.'

Alan suggested helpfully that Six Bits run with a wily veteran hound as example, and hopes were raised as the pair set off with purpose. 'Go boy!' entreated Pete. 'Go Six Bits!' Then: 'Oh, you soft cock!'

Six Bits had abruptly broken stride, sought unsuccessfully to persuade his rival of the futility of the exercise, then darted into a shed to drop another steamer. Cradling Six Bits back to the kennel, Alan confided, 'If shitting was racing, this dog'd win everything in sight.'

'Is there any category of racing he might be suited to?' I asked.

DK answered for him: 'Category One Bullet.'

It's not quite so bad. Six Bits still has a lot of support round the Yarras—Pete Macca's brother Rod has designated his fantasy league team 'The Save Six Bits Fund'—and there have been expressions of interest about him as a pet.

In my role as Yarras chairman of selectors, I've also offered Six Bits some counselling. 'We think you're a good player out of luck. Reckon you'll do better in the lower grades.' As for funding the Yarras from our punting fortunes, we may have to go down the scale a bit. Luckily, our player list includes a couple of stockbrokers.

Week 24

Veterans

Beachcomber's classic definition of 'bombshell' as 'the exclusion of a cricketer from a cricket team' has stood the test of time in Australia. Refugee crises and miscellaneous wars on terror have seemed paltry indeed since Steve Waugh's retrenchment from the national one-day XI on Wednesday.

It's the perfect news story, in a sense, for the 'Big Temptation Survivor' era of ritualised humiliation. Mike Munro's 'I-Feel-Your-Pain' interview on 'A Current Affair' was all one could have hoped for.

'Tell me, Steve, how do you feel?'

'Pretty bad.'

'You must feel pretty bad.'

'I do.'

'That's pretty bad.'

'It is.'

Perhaps Trevor Hohns should have appeared at the press conference gussied up as Cornelia Francis: 'You are the Weakest Link. Goodbye.'

At the Yarras, the bombshell was greeted with incredulity. Too old? At thirty-six? By our lights, Waugh hasn't even attained mellow maturity let alone wily veteranhood. Providing he didn't take over karaoke night with one of those excruciating John Williamson songs that he likes, we'd happily toss him a lifeline. Slats, a veritable colt at thirty-two, could come as well, though he'd have to cop being bagged about that dumb tattoo.

It's the nature of park cricket that participants are a little dimmer of eye and longer in tooth than average. This isn't a staging post, it's a mooring—and in time maybe a drydock and breaker's yard as well. Personally, I'm quite content with that. As the baseballer Frank Sullivan put it: 'I'm in the twilight of a mediocre career.' But others with a few years on the clock, by contrast, are coming into their own. Two blokes who seem to embody this are One Dad and Thommo, key bowlers under the sage skippership of Doc in the Thirds.

One Dad is forty-two, tall, broad-shouldered, bespectacled and bald as a coot. He is, as mentioned, a Christian who celebrates each wicket with a hearty 'Hallelujah!' and who declines to play Sundays. He's also a latecomer to cricket, who discovered the game only five years ago and taught himself to bowl fast.

I respect that. Had I been in One Dad's position, I'd have set my sights a little lower, perhaps promoting myself as a specialist fly slip. But no, One Dad wanted a crack at breaking his back, like an accountant suddenly deciding he'd like to work as an astronaut. He has a red hot go, too.

I'll often stop at training simply to savour One Dad's approach. It's entirely untutored, and thus in each respect somewhat exaggerated, like a fast-bowling mime. After sidling in a few strides, he starts pumping his arms like he's trying to elbow through a crowd, and his little French impressionist's beard tightens in a moue of anticipation. He then holds the ball aloft, as though offering the batsman an early warning should they wish to run away, and launches at the crease, uncoiling his bowling arm like a catapult—at considerable speed, because he's as strong as an ox, and with an appreciable away swing.

Still a kid in cricket terms, moreover, One Dad is overwhelmingly eager for advice. He refers to me as Obi-Wan for my alleged sagacity; in fact, he's become such a good player that I wish I could remember everything I've told him. One Dad, furthermore, adores batting, and spends ages trying to parlay promotions from number eleven to number ten, so that he can unleash his one shot—the sweep. Cricket, of course, isn't One Dad's religion—religion is his religion—but his is the zeal of the convert.

Thommo, One Dad's foil, is forty. He's a cop, and looks like one: craggy, slightly austere, with the economy of his words matching the general economy of his mouth—of which he only ever uses a corner, and then never for long. Thommoisms are succinct and flavoursome. A few weeks ago, the Thirds were passing round a copy of '*FHM*'s top hundred babes', and solicited Thommo's opinion of Sarah O'Hare. 'Ya wouldn't kick her out of bed for farting,' he mused.

Thommo is the archetypal 'set-and-forget' medium pacer, uncomplaining and inexhaustible, purveying cunning breaks that are never quite there to hit—it's like slashing at a handful of confetti. And I began to appreciate just how much it means to him to play when, some months ago, he revealed a little personal history.

Over a decade ago, Thommo was severely injured in an accident in which his wife died. Another driver lost control and crossed a median strip to collide with their car, head-on. Doctors did the best they could for his mangled left knee in a series of operations, and Thommo restored his mobility by taking up ballroom dancing, finishing third in the state titles and eventually becoming an instructor. Within a few years, he was bowling again at his old club, Burnley. He traditionally bowled half the season's overs, simply plugging away unchanged from one end.

One Dad and Thommo: it never fails to gladden my heart when I pop into Como Park to watch the Thirds, and chance on them at opposite ends, with their vastly different styles and stories. Take it from me, Steve, you can get a game here anytime you like.

Week 25

Catches

Cricket is replete with annoying truisms. Which may be a good thing, as it allows otherwise unemployable ex-cricketers to spend their twilight years observing how that 697 in the fourth innings is 'a big ask', and how you can't bowl *there* to Brian Lara.

Most resilient among truisms, though, must be 'catches win matches'. It's great that commentators still utter this expression as if it is part of some mystical cabbala known only to the Knights of the Jedi. *'Great catch! And, as they say, catches win matches.' 'By Jove, there's a lot in that.'*

Well, yes, up to a point. Taking a catch clearly doesn't harm anyone's cause. But while watching the Yarras Fourths turf another ten chances at the weekend on the way to victory by an innings and fifty runs, I reflected that we've given the old catches–matches correlative a pretty solid drubbing of late.

The fact is that we've dropped some absolute gobbers. The best was a one-hander that Pete Macca spilt at long-off during our AB Memorial Match a month ago; it was a one-hander because he was placing a bet with the mobile phone in his other hand. Pete was spared greater mockery because the horse came in at very lucrative odds—others have collected nothing at all.

And yet, we've been cleaning up. Our Seconds, Thirds and Fourths are strolling into the sunny uplands of finals; the Fourths are perched atop their league ladder despite having a cordon that takes the designation slip literally and which has held one catch for the entire season (a rebound). It's not a formula you'd recommend, and I suspect a few more will have to stick in due course, but it's working for us.

In big cricket, fielding errors are notoriously destructive of morale. Drop a catch in a Test and you can be sure there are ten other guys thinking, 'I coulda caught that between the cheeks of my arse.' But the lower the standard, the greater the pathos in putting one down. Drop a catch at the Yarras, and ten teammates will be reflecting privately, 'Phew. Glad that didn't come to me.'

The missing of a catch can even be rather endearing. Womble pursuing an airborne ball is like a character in a Chuck Jones cartoon. The will oozes, the legs pump, and the body arrives hopelessly late with an accompanyingly elaborate excuse (such as, 'I thought the ball was spinning clockwise, but it was actually anti-clockwise').

A favourite moment this season involved Scotty, a classy young quick who works as a schoolteacher. Late last year, he described to us idioms of modern report-writing. There are, he explained, no 'bad' children any more. The bonehead incapable of counting to ten 'may benefit from revision in order to fulfil his potential'. The brat who defiantly refuses instruction 'may need to restrain his otherwise commendable initiative'.

A couple of hours later, I was at mid-off while Scotty bowled a testing spell, culminating in a bouncer that looped from a top edge towards Womble at square leg. Womble's arms extended and his legs started moving, apparently very fast, but not very far, as though on an invisible treadmill.

He went one way. Then he went another. He came

forward. He scuttled back. He probably finished in his original position, only scanter of breath. The ball descended to earth half a metre away. As grown men wiped away tears of laughter, Scotty sighed: 'Lapses in concentration may have led to some gaps in comprehension.'

Myself? I can claim to have caught all the important ones; i.e. the caught and bowleds. But I've also outdone all my comrades this season in being the only Yarras player to drop a girl. Or, to be precise, Mary, who is an institution in our otherwise extremely butch competition.

Mary plays for Burnley. In fact, she's played a hundred games for the Burners, is more than handy in the field, and never fails to excite a cheer when she obtains a run at number 11. She loves cricket, and I'm full of admiration for her. In fact, on the relevant day, my admiration had induced something of a reverie: 'Marvellous, really. Girl playing cricket. Takes you back. Days of innocence. Youthful high spirits. Jumpers for wickets. Mmmm, that looks like a cricket ball coming towards me. Errr, now it's on the grass.'

Apparently—I must here take the word of others—it was a gentle full toss and a gentler top edge. So in hindsight, it's a shame I didn't pick the ball up and hurl four overthrows, thus making the episode a candidate for the most incompetent passage of play in cricket history—when you're in a position like that, you might as well go for broke.

I was reminded of dropping Mary when I bumped into the Burnley boys again at the weekend, who cheerfully dared me to write about it (that's that taken care of). And, on reflection, it's no wonder commentators indulge in so many platitudes. They no longer have to live up to them.

Week 26

Crisis

It used to be said that the back page of the newspaper chronicled only man's successes, the front page only failures. That can hardly be true any more. The front pages aren't rosier, but the back pages are discernibly gloomier.

These days the headlines shriek at you: 'CORRUPTION SCANDAL', 'FINANCIAL CRISIS', 'RELEGATION BATTLE'. And these things don't only matter at the big end of town. Although inured to corruption scandals by having nothing worth corrupting, the Yarras have just faced a financial crisis and a relegation battle—in the one weekend.

The financial crisis was fully anticipated. In fact, we have one so often at this time of year that I could write in my diary for March 2003 right now: 'Yarras to suffer financial crisis (practise grovelling).' We tend to cruise for most of the season on a zero bank balance, operating as a kind of conduit through which money passes on the way to councils, curators, associations, makers of cricket balls and distributors of alcoholic beverages.

Imaginative accounting usually sees us through. If Fat Tony, our treasurer, was CFO at Enron, it would still rank high in the *Fortune* 500. But as far as building reserves is concerned, it's a little like trying to get off the mark at the weekend, then arriving at the other end to find the umpire signalling leg byes...all afternoon. And around March, margin for financial error narrows, and an informal policy of austerity operates. Second new ball? Why not just get a bit more wear out of that first one? After all, it's still red, isn't it?

Hence the trivia night which, in the Yarras social calendar, follows our karaoke evening (barbecue plus singing) and seven-a-side tournament (barbecue plus slogging). This can make the difference between having next to no money at the end of the season and no money at all—and that's quite a difference. I suggested holding such an event four years ago when I'd still to grasp the Yarras principle that those who suggest, do. Thus I've run it for the last four years, latterly with TB, whose schmoozing charms are seldom better exhibited.

This year, we showed the benefit of some experience, in some unexpected areas. We'd all been looking forward to trivia night, but perhaps not quite as much as Moof. When I found myself behind him in the food queue, he confided, 'Think I might set a new record tonight, chairman.'

'Points?' I asked.

'No,' he replied. 'Plates. I'm very hungry. I haven't eaten since lunchtime.'

An ill omen. A couple of years ago, Moof returned to the carvery so frequently that an entire table went unfed. Now I kept him occupied by explaining the structure of the questions, intriguing him with the rounds designated 'Stuff Girls Know' and 'Stuff Boys Know'.

'There should be a round called "Stuff Moof Knows",' he contended. 'You know, menu items from McDonald's, kinds of pizza.' We tried to imagine a round in which only he would be able to collect a perfect ten. Question: If you ordered minestrone, cannelloni, main course lasagne, salad, garlic bread and 1.5 litres of Coke at Tamani's, would you also be able to fit in the tira misu with cream and ice cream? Answer: Yes. Strategically distracted, Moof let two whole tables of people squeeze past him.

As the setter of questions, I always find it fascinating to discover what is now common and uncommon knowledge. A couple of years ago, I asked what I considered a bog standard cricket question: Who had said 'there are two teams out there and one of them is trying to play cricket'? Bill Woodfull's immortal Bodyline rebuke produced not a flicker of recognition.

This year, however, there were some breathtaking gets. 'Me and Me Bitches'—a table featuring Pete Macca and various associated belles—were simply unbeatable on the 'Stuff Girls Know', questions culled largely from the pages of *New Weekly*. They even knew that Jennifer Lopez had bought Cris Judd two pairs of Gucci sterling silver handcuffs from a New York sex shop. 'Hartigan's Heroes', on which McFly had gathered the three other captains, Dave Macca, Doc and Churchyard, looked on in awe. You could see them thinking: So that's what it takes to skipper the Firsts.

During the 'Strange But True' round, meanwhile, Rasputin's 'Rasta Nuns of the Revelations' showed an uncanny acquaintance with the contents of my *Ripley's Believe It or Not Annual 1975* and *Panati's Extraordinary Origins of Everyday Things*. I was also forced to wonder whether the duration of a pig's orgasm had somehow been a memorable subplot on *All Creatures Great and Small*.

TB presided brilliantly over the paper plane endurathon, which DK won with a certainty betokening years of experimentation with the contents of the office stationery cabinet. The raffles then produced sensations. Freakishly, a Rasta Nun won both of the Shiatsu massages at Richmond's Japanese Bathhouse. Still more freakishly, the $100 dinner voucher to The Keg in Albert Park was collected by Moof. Arms thrust aloft jubilantly as though celebrating a hat-trick, he tugged the envelope from my hand before I had a chance to distract him again. I only hope that with a paltry $100 on offer, he doesn't have to stop at McDonald's on the way home.

'What's the secret?' I asked Pete Macca when 'Me and Me Bitches' prevailed for the second consecutive year. 'Secret?' he replied. 'It's those girls. Jeez, they're competitive. I just sit on my arse and keep the drinks coming.' He took the same approach into the following day's relegation battle.

To avoid demotion, our Firsts had to avoid losing to second-placed Hampton at Hampton, defending a mere 131, albeit on a huge, slow oval. From the far-away Fourths fixture, Womble and I took turns ringing every half-hour, each time encountering a voicemail rebuff. Finally, Pete rang back, and wrung every last bit of drama from the occasion.

'G'day chairman.'

'What's the story?'

'They were 6-35...'

'Uh-huh.'

'...then they were 6-111...'

'O-oh.'

'...then 8-131...'

'Crikey.'

'...and Humphrey took wickets with consecutive balls.'

'Are you telling me that we tied?'

'We tied.'

'Did you have to do anything yourself?'

'Nope. Just like trivia night.'

The knot of Fourths players trying to interpret my expression exchanged stupefied glances then exultant expletives. In all, it was a landmark weekend for the Yarras: solvency re-established, indignity avoided. Like I said, who needs the headlines when you're privy to such weekly drama? Behind the six-point nonpareil in which the *Age* prints the weekend's club cricket scores lie stories that are, except in financial terms, far, far richer.

Week 27

Finals

At the Yarras we never predict anything, and, as Gazza would say, never will. But we begin the season's concluding stages sustained by familiar dreams and unfamiliar possibilities.

Our summer has reached a triple witching hour: the Second, Third and Fourths XIs this week begin their finals campaigns, the latter two from the unexpectedly lofty vantage of atop their respective ladders. We know what's required—everything that we haven't done in all our previous finals appearances. We also know that picking and preparing the teams will require courage, conviction and enormous wisdom: wonder if we can borrow some.

Selection has been a hot topic at the Yarras for the

last three weeks—or Australian selection has anyway. Steve Waugh's one-day redundancy has been roundly condemned. Just who does Trevor Hohns think he is? Fancy appointing a mediocre slow bowler to act as chairman of selectors for Australia! Hmmm...as the mediocre slow bowler who acts as chairman of selectors for the Yarras, I can't help sensing some vague parallels being drawn.

Chairmen of selectors always know when finals are imminent. Guys want to buy you drinks. Guys want to remind you of drinks they've bought you in the past. They're right behind you *all the way*. They know you face *tough decisions*. No one confronts their own position issue directly, but it's such a shame that Lefty's never been able to hit the ball off his legs, and that Donger's back plays up whenever the wind changes. Oh, you didn't know...?

If you're a chairman of selectors, you might as well savour this brief uptick in popularity. It's similar to the opinion polls at the start of US presidential cycles that show huge followings for the likes of Steve Forbes and Pat Buchanan. And just as Forbes and Buchanan are always washed up by Super Tuesday, you'll be a pariah by Selection Thursday.

To their credit, the guys know how competitive selection will be in these next few weeks. Some have even made pre-finals sacrifices. Had sacrifices been solicited last season, a few blokes might have promised to give up the reverse sweep for Lent, and then only half-heartedly. Now they're lining up. Big John, our resident pothead, will be renouncing his usual joint before batting. McFly, our resident pantsman, has dumped both the girls he's been shagging. And One Dad, our resident Christian, has relaxed his policy of never playing Sundays. 'God understands finals,' he maintains.

Preparing for finals, however, has never been a Yarras specialty. In my first finals series I was skippered by Lombard—Lots Of Money But A Real Dickhead—of dreadful memory. His captaincy was compounded of cliches and homilies, such as 'there is no "I" in team', or 'there are eleven players in a cricket team, and eleven letters in the word co-operation'. It wasn't clear whether he was captaining cricket or Scrabble.

Lombard particularly floored us one day with a rallying speech that concluded, 'There once was a man who was angry because he had no shoes. Then he met a man who had no feet.'

'I don't get it,' said McFly. 'Does he want us to take our shoes off?'

'No,' Wasim mused, 'I think he wants us to stop bowling no balls.'

As it turned out, we flopped in a semi-final, shoelessness giving way to footlessness before Lombard could make the necessary adjustments.

With the next finals series, our then-coach Waldo took another approach: a John Buchananesque think tank. This involved overhead projections about such minutiae as our rate of singles per hundred balls and the unnoticed correlation between leg byes and the tides, followed by a Rockyesque video of the Australian boxer Kostya Tszyu.

This also bemused us. The positive suggested that there was much to learn from Hulk Hogan, too. The sceptical wondered whether Kostya would be training for his fights by watching videos of the Yarras. Our Firsts and Seconds lost their grand finals, probably unsure whether to dance or rope-a-dope.

As Doc gathered together the Thirds for a pep talk before their grand final last year, One Dad proposed the ultimate premeditation. He produced his Bible, suggesting a silent prayer and an inspirational reading.

Doc hummed and hawed. Castaway, unreconstructed hippy that he is, said that if One Dad could read from the Bible, he was entitled to read from Herman Hesse. The idea fell on stony ground. So did ten chances; Doc's boys, it seemed, were incapable of putting their hands together for any purpose. It turned out that the name of Our Lord Jesus Christ was invoked quite a lot that day—though not as One Dad had envisioned.

None of this, it must be said, augurs well. Philosophy, science, religion—all have failed us. On the other hand, it leaves us no choice. We may just have to start playing cricket.

Week 28

Losing

Aussie Gen-Xers, especially those whose upbringings were so dull all they had to do on Sunday was watch television, will remember the portentous intro to ABC's 'Wide World of Sports'. Its refrain about 'the thrill of victory and the agony of defeat' is part of the soundtrack of our lives, although I wondered even then whether it made better rhetoric than sense.

It can, for sure, hurt to lose, as indeed we just have. A week after the boom in the fortunes of the Yarras Firsts, the boom has descended on the Yarras Seconds in their semi-final meeting with Ajax Maccabi. The Thirds and Fourths live to fight another day, and so do Dave Macca's boys—but in six months' time.

Dave Macca's surpassed himself in leading the

Seconds into the finals this year; but then, he's done a lot of self-surpassing since he arrived. Until his brothers Pete, Steve and Rod beguiled him to join the Yarras, thirty-eight-year-old Dave had played no higher standard than the Macca backyard (mind you, if their training etiquette is a guide, there'd have been no gimmes there). His technique is no thing of beauty, but he is a hard competitor—perhaps he was a disciple of ABC's 'Wide World of Sports' too. Dave's wife Mel once told me that when he settles down to watch his footy club Essendon play on television—this ritual being associated with extensive shouting, whooping and fist-slamming—the family dog retreats to the corner and cowers.

Dave also likes other competitors with old-fashioned values. This became evident at selection on the Thursday before the semi. Green Eye, a gritty middle-order batsman and ex-Seconds captain, had been unavailable for some weeks because of work. And while we've tended hitherto to dismiss his engineer's job as glorified ditch-digging, he must do something quite important, because it had recently entailed him commuting to and from Kuala Lumpur. Or he's a drug courier. Whatever.

With finals in the air, though, Green Eye did what every good club man does: throw all other aspects of his life into chaos in order to play. 'I've told the boss that I've got to come back on Thursday for very important personal reasons,' he told Dave Macca. 'So I'll be at training. And I'm available for the weekend.'

The last batting spot came down to Panther or Green Eye. Panther: social secretary, stylish strokemaker. Green Eye: respected veteran, reliable grafter. Romantic Pete Macca preferred style: 'I dunno guys. Panther always looks a million bucks to me.' Pragmatists Dave Macca and myself plumped for substance. 'Call it intuition if you like,' averred Dave, 'but I think Green Eye's the man for the big occasion.' I agreed. 'My heart says Panther, but my head says Green Eye.' Green Eye made a quacker, dropped a gobber and was back digging his KL ditch the next day. On reflection, picking a player who had virtually to pass through passport control wearing his pads may have been a bit optimistic.

There was, I might add, no hint of favouritism, even in the contest between my heart and head. Both Panther *and* Green Eye feature in the Hesketh Naylers, my Yarras Fantasy League XI; thus I collected zero points from the transaction. With such unerring judgment, plus the rule that you have to include yourself, it's no wonder the Hesketh's finished the competition this week well out of the money.

Rhino topped the Fantasy League, his Legoland Plastic XI edging out Humphrey's Heroes thanks to plenteous runs from Steve Macca, CC and McFly and bumper wicket harvests by Thommo, Castaway and One Dad. Rhino accepted the honour with due humility: 'I'd like to thank all the members of the Legoland XI. The astronaut, the pirate, the policeman, the construction worker...'

'What about the Red Indian?' I interjected.

'You're thinking of the Village People,' Rhino stated firmly.

My suggestion that the winner of Fantasy League automatically become chairman of selectors, becoming the Laurent Kabila to my Mobutu Seko Sese, was also firmly quashed. 'We want guys to try and *win* Fantasy League,' commented Pete. 'Not regard it as method of meting out punishment.'

Pete was involved in another complicated set of calculations during the semi-final. As DK went out to bat with three zeroes behind him this season, I reminded him that the least-coveted Yarras trophy was still up for grabs: the Ducks Award. *Treasure Island* had the 'black spot' to fill men with dread; at the Yarras, a plastic Kahlua duck collected by our former secretary Whispers on a drinking tour of New Zealand and nailed to a plank casts a similar spell.

Nothing much disturbs DK's beatitude, but the smile that crossed his face was an uneasy one. Five minutes later he passed in the opposite direction with an altogether darker expression, Bloodbath having called him for a quick single that a batsman on horseback wouldn't have negotiated safely.

As DK's bat clattered round the concrete walls of the dressing room, Pete's face lit up: 'Four ducks, I believe. Same as me.' As club statistician, he set to work with his various tie-break mechanisms—least number of innings, higher nominal position in batting order, dismissals by bowlers etc. Painstaking stuff.

'Any answer?' I asked finally. 'Nah, it's no good,' answered Pete. 'No matter which method I use, I still win it.'

Agony of defeat for Dave, thrill of victory for Rhino,

thrill of defeat for DK, agony of victory for Pete. In other words, another full, rich Yarras weekend—altogether fuller and richer than those I clearly wasted in watching ABC's 'Wide World of Sports'.

Week 29

Winning

My friend Darky is getting married in Brisbane at Easter. Around 5 p.m. last Sunday, I rang him from Melbourne's Fawkner Park to apologise in advance for my absence. 'Waddya mean?' he said. 'It's the biggest day of my life.'

'Mine, too,' I said. 'I'll be playing in a grand final.'

'All right,' he responded, 'you're in the clear.'

The Yarras' Third and Fourth XIs have both made it all the way. The Thirds gave their semi-final opponents short shrift; the Fourths offered theirs extensive shrift in a game bound to go down in club annals, should 'annalling' ever occur.

Selection was tense for, coincidentally, other matrimonial reasons. Doc, our Thirds skipper, wanted to drop One Dad. I disagreed. The situation was made awkward because we're both going to One Dad's wedding in April. (One Dad is sensible enough to be getting married *after* the season is over). Finally, I gave in. Doc had better come up with a good present next month.

Only when the teams were read out did Wonder Dog Two inform us that Ghost, our best young batsman, was unavailable on the appointed day: he was heading for a twenty-first birthday party in the bush. Dammit dammit dammit! Churchyard double-checked this by ringing Ghost. 'He says he would have rung us,' Churchyard reported, 'but he lost his mobile.' A look of dawning awareness then crossed Churchyard's face. 'Hang on. I just rang him on his bloody mobile…'

A panicky ring around led us to Denny, a club stalwart but infrequent player since family responsibilities encroached on his time. When we pledged to work around his need to leave at 5 p.m. on Saturday and 2 p.m. on Sunday, he consented. He awaited his innings dandling a gleeful toddler on one padded knee, and pushing a pram containing a dozing infant back and forth with a gloved hand.

Our opponents had the ecclesiastical name Emmanuel, although there weren't many altar boys in evidence. They sledged fulsomely and didn't mind throwing the odd punch—among themselves anyway. This appeared to be their method of sorting out a batting order.

We then had the problem that Torqs, our best fast bowler and biggest management challenge, was nowhere to be found. This was not surprising: another of Torqs' characteristics is that he usually arrives hotfoot, cursing constipated traffic and erratic alarm clocks as the umpire declares 'Play'. But his absence so close to start time now compelled Churchyard to bat on winning the toss, and in helpful conditions we were restricted to 124.

Although Torqs arrived in time to bat, he then completely blew a gasket on taking the new ball. (Since his tribunal appearance, he had bowled brilliantly and behaved impeccably, if never with complete ease—it's been like watching like 'Chopper' Read at an elocution lesson.) Once again he ran foul of his umpiring nemesis Pat Pending: a few operatic calls of 'BAAALLL!!' and Torqs was as innocuous as an album by All Saints—although the language was a bit worse.

Emmanuel's star batsmen Blacksmith and Billy Ray Cyrus—as we codenamed them for their technical and tonsorial attributes respectively—began in a blaze of brilliant strokes, blind slogs and excruciating edges. Rhino took wing as one projectile entered his airspace at point...then plummeted to earth like a shot duck. On landing, his knee emitted a noise usually associated with a tree under the axe. Had it been a Test match, he'd have been surrounded by doctors, physios, paramedics, and his ghost writer; as this was the Yarras, his horrified wife ran on while we made our considered communal diagnosis: 'Reckon yer knee's rooted, mate.'

Fortunately, we had One Dad. Of someone whose Bible is *The* Bible, it would be inappropriate to say he bowled like a demon; still irked with Doc, he was more your avenging angel.

Blacksmith was bowled all over the place. 'Hallelujah!' One Dad exulted. 'Praise the Lord!'

Billy Ray flailed a drive so hard that, with no time to clear the way at mid-off, I was obliged to catch it. With Wogger bowling manfully in support, then batting obstinately, we were able to set our rivals 170.

By that time, sans Rhino and Denny, we were an IX rather than an XI. This entailed a rota of six substitutes, rostered for an hour here and there according to other engagements, including the mercurial Larry.

Young Larry is a singular character, even at the Yarras. He was a bit of a teenage tearaway. In his high school yearbook, he listed as his ambition: 'To die on a motorcycle.' Now in his early twenties, a factory hand and rave DJ, he spends a fair chunk of time off the field in pharmacological La-La Land. Luckily, though, he regards cricket as the most fun possible that's legal. He has a majestic pull shot, an enormous off-break delivered with an action that makes Muralitharan's appear the acme of orthodoxy, and a fast, flat throw that causes keepers to quail.

Billy Ray learned this the hard way, after starting the second innings with a couple of arrogant boundaries, then attempting a hubristic single to cover. He'd barely crossed when Larry's return detonated the stumps. Blacksmith then prodded to mid-off amid rousing cheers from the crowd.

Notice how cunningly I've introduced that there was a crowd, as though this is standard for Yarras games. Actually, we seldom attract more than the two ageing hippies who stand by the Como Park boundary waiting for us to finish so they can throw their frisbee. But on this occasion there were spectators, not only Doc and the Thirds, who'd finished their game early, but thirty or so other clubmates, family and friends. Nine-year-old Mitch, whose enjoyment of cricket somehow survived watching forty freezing overs of Boxing Day Test cricket with me at the MCG, joined his sister in shrieks of 'Go Yarras!' Rasputin's girlfriend had erected a banner in his honour—'Rasputin: Never Say Die!' Even Torqs perked up—when Churchyard put him on at the opposite end.

When the last wicket fell, a happy throngette surrounded the pitch. 'I've never seen so many Yarras people in the one place,' confided TB, the club president. 'We should probably hold the annual meeting.'

I asked if I could borrow his phone. 'This'll sound a bit strange, TB,' I replied. 'But I've got a wedding to get out of.'

Week 30

Anticipation

Shopping for a wedding gift this week, I elected to buy Darky and his bride the *Shorter Oxford English Dictionary*. A simple enough task, one might think. But no.

The *Shorter OED* comes in two volumes: A-M and N-Z. And this completely confounded the bookshop assistant. Did I really want both? There were, after all, words in each one. My explanation that the volumes each contained different words was considered unsatisfactory: after all, how many words does a person need? I had either the world's most obtuse bookshop assistant, or the deepest. I placated her only by revealing that the volumes were a wedding present. Now she understood. One for him, and one for her.

The dialogue was only slightly more fanciful than the argy-bargy over Doc's and Churchyard's respective grand final sides. If the Thirds had A and B, did it really need C, when D was also available, and E could be relied on at a pinch? If the Fourths had C, alternatively, might spots be kept for F, G and H? And might I be free to retire a happy chairman?

Queasily conscious of the coming showdown, I'd been permutating teams idly on the backs of envelopes and bills and trying them out on Trumper the cat for some weeks. But complications were steadily multiplying. 'I'm pretty good really,' Rhino said when I checked on his condition. 'Just dealt with the Nazi hordes for the third time today.' This was a reference to a computer game with which he was amusing himself at home rather than unexpected good news about his mobility; in fact, with his anterior cruciate ligament snapped and his patella dislocated, cyber-stormtroopers had best beware.

Next it was Denny. In return for his semi-final leave pass, he'd promised his wife an Easter weekend down the coast, and communicated apologetically that he'd be available only the first two days of the final which basically ruled him out. And, outstanding individual performances always being a mixed blessing for subordinate XIs, the Fourths' semi-final matchwinner One Dad would likely be recalled to the Thirds.

Then there were the returnees. Kreuger, having been at a car-wash convention in Sydney during the semi, and Ghost, having been pissed under a tree somewhere, were available again. But both were bound for Wonder Dog Two's twenty-first in Barwon Heads on Saturday evening. Did we trust them all to return in time for the second day? And then Rasputin e-mailed: 'Have to go to my cousin's best friend's maths tutor's 21st in Hoppers Crossing this weekend. Don't know how pissed I'll get. Should be able to turn up for game sometime. Can you work around me?' In case I didn't get it, he sent the supplementary advice, 'Kidding'.

This, too, is merely the executive summary: Thursday night's selection Hansard wouldn't bear perusal. Churchyard wondered aloud why the Thirds needed five experienced new ball bowlers (Moof, Thommo, One Dad, Castaway and Wonder Dog Two), leaving the Fourths with one (the irascible Torqs). Doc was immovable, and Pete and Dave Macca robustly of the view that remaining Fourths players would simply have to 'step up': the Stairmaster school of selection. Unfortunately, some would have to step down as well, specifically Hot Dog, a Thirds regular who'd now find himself in the Fourths, and Big Al, a Fourths stalwart who'd now miss out altogether.

Crikey, how do proper selectors do this? How did they drop Dean Jones, when I felt sick with dread about demoting a vegetarian all-rounder with an eyebrow ring like Hot Dog? Anyway, the deed was done. Although at first he looked like he'd been stabbed in the vitals, Hot Dog bucked up, while big-hearted Big Al even agreed to act as twelfth man for both games.

By Yarras standards this week was rather tense. When I played a shot off my pads at training, which Thommo commented put him in mind of Mark Waugh, I quickly replied, 'Yep, it's time to retire.' To lift my spirits on the way home from an extra net with Doc, One Dad, Watto and CC on Friday evening, I borrowed a video of *Any Given Sunday*. This is Oliver Stone's absurdly histrionic and oddly compelling vision of American football, with Al Pacino as the old-fashioned coach, Jamie Foxx as the cutting-edge quarterback, and Cameron Diaz as the flint-hearted owner, a sort of Gordon Gekkette.

I've never understood the view of Oliver Stone as an anti-establishment moviemaker: I suspect he's a closet conservative. For all the rap and cocaine, *Any Given Sunday* is about as subversive as *The Lou Gehrig Story*. But if you've any feeling for sport, Al Pacino's peroration is pure gold spun from complete corn. And while I don't know whether it inspired me, I awoke on grand final morning with a weird feeling of having just shagged Cameron Diaz.

Grand Final

The Big One

So far, it occurs to me, I've written very little about actual Yarras matches. This isn't all that surprising, as it sometimes seems like we're more a barbecue club with facilities for occasional batting and bowling. But of twin grand finals—Yarras in action, as opposed to Yarras inaction—I can scarcely avoid description. Here's the whole megillah.

Grand final morning feels little different to any other Saturday. I can't find my shirt. One boot is in the hallway, one in the bathroom. Trumper has been curled on my cricket sweater at the foot of the bed, lightly downing it in grey fur. The usual.

I like to read on match mornings, when I'm not answering the phone and responding to questions such as 'Can you organise a sub for the first hour of the Seconds game?', 'Do you know where Gary Smorgon no. 9 Reserve is?', or 'Do you know where the keys are?' (that one's easy: ring Womble). This morning, on the tram to Fawkner Park, I peruse the latest edition of *Best American Sports Writing*, and encounter an interesting essay by Charles Young. 'Losing: An American Tradition' deplores the way that 'loser' has infiltrated the American vernacular as the ultimate damnation, although the real winner's circle in the US is very small indeed. The obsession with winning, Young continues, is as injurious to winners as to losers, as those who win are 'taught that they are good only to the extent that they beat other people'. Right on, Chuck! It then strikes me that this isn't the way Steve Waugh would prepare for a vital Test innings.

It happens that both the grand finals, for Thirds and Fourths, involve games with Powerhouse, and on adjacent grounds. The Yarras caravan is already establishing itself on the grassed area between the two. Womble arrives with the barbecue and Bourkey's custom-built XL esky on wheels—with its distinctive legend 'VB Lives Here'—to ratify our territorial claim. Churchyard and I fetch the kit from his car.

Just to remind us of where this pilgrimage began, AB's pads are lying on top of the team bag: this time a year ago, he was still wearing them, was still captain of the Fourths and reigning club karaoke champion.

Most of the boys have, as requested, arrived an hour before the scheduled 11 a.m. commencement and we compare notes about our respective preparations. 'I had a dream that I scored 300,' reports Hot Dog positively. 'I had a dream I got picked for the Thirds,' Churchyard recalls ruefully.

Ghost is looking like his nickname; his entire generation seems to be turning twenty-one at once, and he confesses to another late shift the night before. Trav Keg, by contrast, had settled for a lower-key preparation. 'I had a very relaxing night, actually,' he says. 'Got laid three times.'

'Was anyone else involved?' I ask.

'Imagination is a powerful thing,' he replies.

The only absentee is Torqs—running, as ever, on Torqs Time. A cricket captain awaiting his players before a game is like a Battle of Britain squadron leader scanning the horizon for his returning Spitfires: 'There's Bertie. There's Biffo. But no sign of Smudger. And it looks like Squiffy's bought it.' Churchyard is straining to retain his stiff upper lip, although more from annoyance than anxiety. Finally, with the toss imminent, he punches Torqs' number into his phone. 'I'm in Nicholson Street!' Torqs replies breathlessly. 'I'm flyin! I'm flyin!'

Churchyard announces this in a long-suffering tone: 'Torqs will be flying in today.' From the nearby hospital, a helicopter passes overhead. 'That could be him now...'

No car keys are required to tell us that the pitch is a belter, and in the tradition of Fawkner Park eccentricities, the boundary to one side is absurdly short and encompasses a row of trees (bowling slow at Fawkner can be torture—I remember a day I was hit into the foliage so often that a teammate got bored with retrieving and lobbed back a pinecone rather than the ball). Torqs' gridlocking forms an additional rationale for batting. 'If we can get through the first hour,' said Churchyard, 'we should be okay.'

At the end of the first hour we're 4-27. Churchyard and Steve Macca, more than 1000 runs between them this season, have totalled 7. Ghost has been woozily yorked. Hot Dog has snicked a wide. Torqs has arrived...just in time to put the pads on. 'Good timing,' he says airily. As it happens, he bats well, and we're glad he troubled to drop in, although our saviour is Wogger, the croupier cricketer. Over the season, we've developed immense respect for Wogger's two shots: the Wogger One, a flat-footed flail through cover, and the Wogger Two, a short-armed tug from outside off stump through mid-wicket. His other virtue is an ability to play and miss with utter insouciance for what seems entire sessions: it's as though he knows that whatever the fortune of the moment, the house always profits. His 77 today is priceless.

The finals are roughly in parallel by mid-afternoon. Thommo rescues the Thirds after their obligatory Yarras collapse, and the air relaxes somewhat. Castaway presides over the barbecue while wearing his pads. Rhino arrives on crutches, showing off the huge green brace in which his leg is now encased. Big Al, our double-duty twelfth man, offers his nifty deckchair, which has a receptacle in one armrest for beer and in the other for cigarettes; that should expedite his recovery. Pete and Dave Macca shoot video for the website. Mitch and Greer, now semi-officially the Yarras junior fan club, arrive with a banner proclaiming 'Yarras Forever', and a chocolate cake with the injunction 'Go Yarras' embossed in Smarties. I'm charged with retrieving the plastic cricketer that adorns the icing, lest they be one short in games of table-top 'Test Match': we all know how annoying it is to begin a game one short...

At the close, our barbecue glows in the gloaming, the festive board groans with fare, and we talk about other things. Pete Macca is pretty excited. That morning he's visited our new greyhound breaker, the Dog Whisperer, to check on Six Bits, whom we've chucked a few more dollars at in the hope of getting him racing—or at least delaying the bullet option. Amazingly, under its new management, Six Bits has been able to complete a full lap of a track. 'Then what was the problem before?' I ask.

'It turns out,' Pete explains, 'that Six Bits was *fat*. You know how greyhounds are meant to be lean? We had the Merv of greyhounds.'

'Funny you should say that. I thought he was carrying a bit of weight when we saw him. But I was too polite to mention it. I thought he might be embarrassed.'

'The good news is that he's lost a lot of weight,' Pete continues. 'He was probably eating too much junk food. Anyway, they've got him down to three pies, four Chiko rolls and a Mars bar a day. I reckon he's an example to the Yarras. His story of sporting redemption will inspire us.'

'I knew we bought him for some reason.'

As chairman of selectors, I probably watch as much cricket at the Yarras as anybody, and will always attend a game I'm not playing where possible. But on the second day of our concurrent, conjoining Fawkner finals, perhaps the most important innings in recent Yarras history is played no more than 100 metres away, and of it I see diddly squat.

Early on, the Thirds make better headway than we do, securing a first innings lead; we drop the usual ration of catches, four of them off me, and are pretty rough in the field. Womble somehow contrives to let a forward defensive stroke toddle to the boundary because he's afraid of running into a tree. Hot Dog at square leg doesn't move to retrieve a leg-side nick because he thinks there's a fine leg who turns out to be One Dad, just outside the boundary, walking back from the toilet. I console myself—because I'm bowling—by recalling the county umpire who called a no ball against Glamorgan for three fielders behind square: leg slip, deep fine, deep square. 'Deep square leg!' roared Wilf Wooller. 'That's a bloody ice-cream vendor!'

Hot Dog is ultimately our hero. It's a hot afternoon, and at times he looks like his wiry figure is going to evaporate in a cloud of sweat, but he secures 7-67, and limits our deficit to 48. Between times, however, everything goes a bit pear-shaped. At the Yarras, we often jest grimly about our propensity for batting collapses. Now we outdo ourselves with consecutive collapses on adjacent ovals. After the Thirds have plummeted in their second innings to 8-65, the Fourths plunge promptly to 3-5. The air is thick with appeals, curses and the sound of ripping velcro. 'Can I borrow your bat?' asks Rasputin as another exultant cry rends the air. 'Errr, now?'

'You need some pads?' Wogger asks Rasputin. 'Use AB's.'

'Are you superstitious, Raz?' I interrupt. 'If so, let me warn you that I've been lbw five times in those pads this season.'

'That's funny,' says Wogger. 'I was out lbw first ball the first time I wore those pads, too. But I wasn't using them when you ran me out. Or when I ran you out.'

'That's because *I* was,' I point out. And we all look at each other, like Cluedo players who've realised simultaneously that Mr Mustard did it.

Withal, even as the Fourths are doing a Humpty Dumpty, the Thirds are putting themselves back together again. Moof is dynamic. Nothing worries him, although occasionally he confides in his partner: 'The bowling's easy. But gee, I could murder a steak.' One Dad, having finally secured a promotion to number 10, shows the patience of Job (he'll like that). After a while, Doc superstitiously forbids anyone to move from their seats—which means that Chilli Dog and I, facing the opposite way to score the Fourths game, see nothing. With a thin screen of small trees separating the two ovals, all we can hear are shouts, applause and the occasional, distant, strangled appeal. Hicksy, perceiving our plight, shouts explanatory advice after each tumult: 'That's the fifty stand', 'That's Moof's fifty', 'Oh, that's one of the most magnificent sixes you will never see!'

Ghost and Churchyard turn it round for the Fourths with a 50 partnership of their own, taking us to and past parity, but with only their dutiful scorers as spectators. I can see Churchyard looking towards our encampment from the middle, as though concerned that everyone else has shot through. In fact, everyone else is urging Moof on to his 100, which duly accrues—I'll have to wait for the video to see how. Womble stokes the barbecue, while everyone basks in Moof's afterglow. The man himself calls his Dad to pass on news of what it emerges is his first century. 'I've always gotten hungry round about the 70s before,' he explains. 'But today I thought about the team.'

'Eating us?' laughs Castaway.

'Beating them,' Moof says, indicating his disconsolate opponents; having penetrated the hungry 70s, the nervous 90s clearly posed no challenge.

The finals are now interestingly poised. The Thirds, first innings win in the bag, can afford a washout on the third day; the Fourths, trailing on first innings, will need every possible over in pursuit of an outright win. 'I suppose,' I venture, 'it's asking too much to expect clear blue skies over one ground and a flood of biblical proportions on the ground next to it.'

'This *is* Melbourne,' Trav Keg observes.

What we get, on the third day, is a bit of everything.

It pours at intervals. It clears at other intervals. We remove the covers to dry the pitch. We replace them to prevent it getting wetter. Seven or eight guys from both sides carry the covers first one way, then the other. It's like watching a flag routine at the Olympic opening ceremony; I half expect to see doves released, or maybe ducks, considering the weather.

The Thirds pitch is mush; ours is a little better, though not much. Ghost and Churchyard get on after an hour...then come straight off, Ghost having blocked one ball, because the run-ups are dicey. When the umps order an early lunch, we can't even get the barbecue lit; Watto solicits orders for McDonald's. 'You know,' Big John recalls, 'this is exactly like our first game this season. Remember how it was bloody freezing and we dropped everything?' Wogger snorts, 'We're still doing that.'

Glancing across the oval towards Powerhouse's club rooms, the Fourths observe a surprising ritual: our opponents posing for a premiership team photo. Hmmm, hubris. Can we provide the necessary nemesis? Everybody tugs their 'AB' caps a little lower. We've fetched from Como Park, at the umpires' behest, a set of rubber bowling mats, and finally a

2 p.m. restart is decreed. Sixty overs are to be bowled. Essentially it's an abbreviated one-dayer which we must win, and Powerhouse need only draw. Batting now isn't easy, with the ball stopping and popping; the pitch soon obtains the consistency of drying bitumen. But Ghost, Churchyard and Rasputin—a slightly spooky trio, now I reflect on it—play tremendously well to steer us to a 120 lead at tea when the declaration is made with forty overs remaining. And after twenty-two overs, Powerhouse are 8-60. Yes, you read that right: 8-60.

Torqs, who is such a good bowler when he channels his energy through the ball rather than his mouth, does really well, on a pitch in the process of drying under what's now a wan sun. It's only a C-Grade premiership, but suddenly the game feels like a Test. New batsmen slouch to the wicket a little sulkily, as though they'd rather be admiring that premiership photo on the wall. Torqs is complemented by Wogger, who offers his usual hearty support. I reckon I can tell from mid-off when Wogger is really bending his back, because his pants slip down a little lower than usual; today he's showing more of his underpants than Tupac Shakur. The other thing I notice from mid-off today is that the surface is bouncing a little lower and more predictably each over. Pitches that have seen a bit of rain make for fascinating cricket. You could plot the course of this game on a three-dimensional graph, with the axes as time, pitch quality, batsmen's ability, bowler's endurance, age of ball etc. Cricket must've contained just such subtle calculations in the days of Trumper. The batsman, not the cat.

By about 5 p.m., Torqs and Wogger have four wickets apiece. But Wogger's a bit worried because he has a classic park cricketer's dilemma: he's on a sickie today, and if he takes five-for, will get his name in the paper.

'Gonna risk it?' I ask.

'I'm pumped mate,' says Wogger. 'Real pumped.' He can feel the crowd behind him: only belatedly do I realise that it's Doc and the Thirds. Their match must be over—in fact, Moof's gone on to 149 not out, and the boys have rolled their rivals outright by 118 runs—but, shamefully, I've hardly given them a thought.

We're lucky to obtain the eighth Powerhouse wicket: their best bat is given out to one of those dreadful bump ball catches, which both teams would describe with sincere and entirely opposite convictions.

I haven't a clue if it's out, but decisions like this make you wince: you feel the same pang of misplaced guilt that you once felt when the headmaster announced at assembly that 'someone' had been smoking behind the sheltersheds, even though it *wasn't* you (you used to do it near the bike racks, and no one ever looked there). The wimp in me wonders whether I will feel good about winning this game.

If we win. Because now, we can't get through. The pitch has settled down. Five, six, seven overs pass, and we can't disturb the ninth-wicket pair, their spinner Hickman and opening bowler Barney. They play grimly, safely and well. Actually, I feel a sneaking admiration for them (*What am I saying?*). Really, there's no reason why these guys don't deserve to win the flag as much as us (*I should never have read that Charles Wright essay! Pull yourself together, man!*). They're OK; they've played good cricket, and in the right spirit (*But not good enough, all right? Come on!*). Hang about, the skipper's coming over. 'Ten overs to go,' Churchyard says. 'What do you think?'

'Keep Torqs going,' I suggest. 'But we need to break up the pattern a bit. Need some variation.' We discuss using Rasputin or Trav Keg. Churchyard manages to extract from me words I don't think I've ever said before: 'Much as I hate to say it, I suspect I should have a trundle.' And I *do* hate saying it but, well, it might do the trick. Cometh the hour, cometh the hack. 'Next over, far end,' says Churchyard. When I take the ball, I hear Hicksy bawling, 'Come on, Sis!'

If this was fiction, I would now claim those last couple of wickets. If this was Hollywood, the decisive catch would be taken by Trumper the cat. As this is a diary, we lose. Yes, Torqs and I bowl out the last ten overs. No, we don't break through. There are some reasonable appeals. Our keeper Stewy Keg reckons we have Barney stumped, but the ump when he looks up is intent on the ball-counter. No kvetsching, though. The ball turns—maybe too much, which forces me to take a few revs off and have a go from round the wicket—but their pads are impassable. Barney ends up having batted eighteen overs for an unbeaten 0. Good on him. Damn him.

Yes, I'm disappointed. In fact, I'm sort of glad I'm disappointed; it means that Charles Young hasn't scarred me for life. But I'm glad I don't stay disappointed all that long; or, to be more precise, the immediate guttedness curdles into a more manageable chagrin. And walking off the field is actually a strange sensation. I notice that all the Thirds guys walking on to greet us, patting our backs and pumping our hands, are wearing sad expressions. Some of them—Moof, Castaway, Hicksy—look devastated. Thommo puts his arm round my shoulders and says feelingly, 'Bad luck, chairman. You guys almost pulled it off. Gutsy effort to come back the way you did.'

I can only think to say, 'Thanks, mate. Yeah, we had a crack.' Then it occurs to me, 'Hey, Thommo. Have you guys won or what?'

He breaks into a smile. 'Yep. Won it. Won the flag.' And suddenly I'm shaking his hand. I've got *my* arm round *his* shoulders, and I'm congratulating him. Because Thommo is a great guy, in a great team, at a great club. Our club.

Epilogue

Stumps

The second-rate, when you think about it, are much maligned. Being second-rate is still pretty good. In fact, it's usually the best you can hope for, in a world where genuine first-rate anything is a rare commodity.

Or so I'm reflecting later that evening at the Yarras' Como Park celebratory wake. Everyone's in a philosophical mood, so I'm not alone. In his speech to the club on behalf of the Fourths, Churchyard tells us that it's the first time he's managed to coax his German partner to the club rooms. 'My girlfriend Ute,' he says, 'describes cricket as "that stupid game in which silly men in white run around pointlessly".' There are murmurs of guilty assent, mixed with the odd challenge of, 'Yeah. And so?'

Especially philosophical is Doc. Our Thirds captain is probably the smartest guy at the Yarras. He's a barrister in his fifties with a deep social conscience who writes incisive opinion pieces for newspapers about weighty issues of legal practice and civil liberties...who's now off his tits. His speech, which involves a thank-you to every person who has helped him in cricket from the man at the sporting goods depot who sold him his first bat, makes Halle Berry's at the Oscars seem the acme of restraint. It takes a lot of well-aimed peanuts to finally shut him up.

Later we have a conversation in which Doc tries simultaneously to eat a burger, drink a beer, smoke a cigarette and cradle the premiership shield—of which he refuses to let go. 'Interleckchalism?' he proposes, 'iss overrated.'

'Mrs Doc won't be happy when you get home,' I warn him.

He looks at me mischievously. 'She's away. Hee hee hee.'

So in this environment of communal rejoicing individual disappointment doesn't stand a chance; in fact, it's fundamental to the life of a club, or at least of a good club, that vicarious pleasure is as real and solid as personal satisfaction. Hicksy has been at the Yarras for twenty-four seasons and this is his first share in a flag: compared with him, I'm a Tragic-Come-Lately. No one this evening, meanwhile, would mistake Wogger for a loser. The doctor who'd issued his certificate that morning would have been delighted by his recovery, or at least by VB's efficacy in treating cases of non-specific symptom-free one-day diarrhoea. Wogger, full of love for the Yarras, shakes my hand with vigour: 'Great season mate. Just great. Really enjoyed it.' Six times. By the time I leave at 4 a.m., Wogger is sitting on the couch, staring into space, appearing to recite *Finnegans Wake*. Castaway listens with touching solicitude.

'Iss hard to bowl,' Wogger insists. 'When ya bin run over. Know wodeye mean?'

'Very true mate,' agrees Castaway.

'I think iss terrible,' Wogger continues. 'Hmmm. A dog'd be good.'

'Dogs *are* good. No doubt about that.'

Yes, good old dogs. I remember a remark by Damon Hill to the effect that 'the only ones who remember you when you come second are your wife and your dog'. It struck me at the time as an especially cruel verdict on cat-owning bachelors like myself. But there's a reason why Damon Hill goes unmentioned in Harold Bloom's *The Western Canon* or Alain de Botton's *Consolations of Philosophy*—his insights into the human condition are pretty bloody limited. Second-place getters we were. Second-rate cricketers we are. Second-class citizens we're not. Sometimes being second is even recognised.

There's been an ongoing minor subplot at the Yarras, involving our star speed merchant Torqs. A couple of weeks ago it emerged that Churchyard's tact, diplomacy and sheer unctuousness had paid off: Torqs was told he'd won the trophy for the best bowling average in the grade. But in order to retain the title of our number one Management Challenge, Torqs told the association secretary where he could stick the trophy—if not where the sun don't shine, at least a shady spot somewhere nearby. 'Sure, fine, whatever, free country, etc,' said the Yarras committee. But this left the association, and us, with a problem.

In the wee hours of the morning of our celebratory wake, Evo from the Hearters, who sits on the association executive, breezes in for a beer. 'We've been discussing the Torqs thing,' he says. 'We need to present the trophy to someone. But there's a concern that the guy who finished second in the bowling averages wouldn't want to accept it if he knew he wasn't actually top.'

'Obviously that's a personal issue,' I reply. 'The individual concerned would clearly need to have no pride, no shame, and no hang-up about mediocrity. Any idea who it is?'

Evo smirked. 'It's you.'

'You've come to the right man, Evo,' I say. 'I accept on behalf of all second-rate cricketers.'

Reward at last.

Three days elapse. The phone falls quiet. There aren't twenty Yarras-related e-mails clogging my Hotmail account. Guess the committee will have to meet again soonish. Then there'll be presentation night, and eventually the annual meeting. But there's nothing pressing, and for a change I find myself writing something other than the *South Yarra Sentinel*. The phone rings.

'Chairman? G'day. What are you up to?'

'Oh, not much, Moof,' I say. 'Bit of writing.'

'What are you writing about?'

'Actually, I'm knocking out something about a great all-rounder like yourself. W. G. Grace.'

'The fat guy, right? With the beard like Castaway's?'

'Correct. I'll include that in the "Stuff Moof Knows" round for trivia night next year. What's taking up your time at the moment?'

There's a pause. 'Well, not much,' says Moof. 'Work. It's boring. I'm at a bit of a loose end. Suddenly I've got all this time on my hands.'

I sigh. 'Same here. Only six months to go though.'

'Of course,' Moof says, 'we don't *have* to wait that long.' Then hesitantly: 'You…errr…wanna hit at Hawthorn Indoor tomorrow night?'

I don't have to think about this either. 'Done.'

'I'll ring Womble,' says Moof. 'Let's go!'

Acknowledgments

I play cricket, and write about cricket, for fun. But it was far from inevitable that I would write about the cricket I played; on the contrary, I needed some persuasion, for which I'm now exceedingly grateful.

Some chapters in *The Vincibles* first appeared in a column called 'A Lot of Hard Yarra' in the *Guardian* in the UK. For that unexpected opportunity I owe a sizeable drink to Ben Clissitt, that newspaper's sports editor. He made the idea—'Why don't you write us some stuff about your club?'—sound as natural as respiration. And so it became.

Thanks are also extended to Graham Coster at Aurum Press, who, on the basis of the foregoing envisioned a book of the Yarras season, has spent the last few months patiently absorbing such peculiarly Australian concepts as Eddie McGuire. At Text Publishing—where I've been even longer than at the Yarras—I acknowledge the accumulated kindnesses of Michael Heyward, Melanie Ostell, Donica Bettanin, Emily Booth, Patty Brown and George Thomas.

Knowingly and unknowingly, the following also contributed to *The Vincibles*: Philippa Hawker, critic, confidante and mother of the unofficial Yarras Junior

Fan Club, Mitch and Greer; Amanda Smith, whose wise advice improved this manuscript just as her outstanding chocolate crackles raised the standard of our afternoon teas; Jason Evans and Rosie Walton of 3RRR's 'Feelin' Kinda Sporty', who made Thursday nights last season noteworthy for reasons other than selection; John Harms, whose wedding came second to my grand final, and who was very decent about it; Robyn Campbell of the Melbourne Headshot Company, wife of Andy (One Dad), whose photograph of our Thirds premiership team adorns the cover; Pete Macaulay, Dave Macaulay and Andrew Walton of ResultsVault, without which I'd have an even weaker grasp of what happened last season; Michael Shatin, who earned my abiding gratitude when he lured me to Como Park in the first place; and Sally Warhaft, who looks forward to the 2002–3 season with anticipation nearly as great as mine.

The chief debt of gratitude, of course, is owed to my clubmates at the Yarras, most of whom appear between these covers. I've used nicknames to protect innocent and guilty alike, but they know who they are. They might obtain from this book a sense of how much pleasure their company has given me over the last nine years. Thanks fellas. Go you good things.

Also by Gideon Haigh

THE BIG SHIP:
WARWICK ARMSTRONG AND THE MAKING OF MODERN CRICKET

Warwick Armstrong remains the only captain in Ashes history to clean-sweep a series, when in 1920–21, as a twenty-one-stone mountain of a man, he won all five Tests. Armstrong lived through a formative period in Australian cricket, when administrators took control of a game which the players themselves had run. Regarded by its new governors as the ultimate nuisance, he proved the great survivor, the Big Ship who was unsinkable.

'In a word: riveting.'
Herald Sun

'The first time I met Gideon Haigh, he was wearing a cricket sweater with a button pinned to it that said, "I support Yorkshire cricket". This affection for a country known for its single-minded players makes him ideal to write about Warwick "Big Ship" Armstrong, one of Australia's most successfully stubborn captains.'
Ian Chappell, *Bulletin*

'A serious story, impressively told, impeccably presented.'
Walter Gammie, *The Times*

448pp, illus, hardback, rrp$60, ISBN 1 876485 98 1